ARMS CONTROL AND DEFENSE: WHO DECIDES?

Volume IX

W. Alton Jones Foundation Series on Arms Control

Edited by Kenneth W. Thompson

University Press of America

Lanham • New York • London

The Miller Center

University of Virginia

Library of Congress Cataloging-in-Publication Data

Arms control and defense.
(W. Alton Jones Foundation series on arms
control ; v. 9)
1. Nuclear arms control—United States.
2. Nuclear arms control—Soviet Union. I. Thompson,
Kenneth W., 1921–   . II. Series.
JX1974.7.A6723   1988 327.1'74'0973   88–26089
ISBN 0–8191–7192–1 (alk. paper)
ISBN 0–8191–7193–X (pbk. : alk. paper)

DEDICATED

TO

PAUL A. THOMPSON

Table of Contents

Preface

Most discussions of arms control focus on ideas and institutions. The rationale for such an approach may go back to Lord Keynes' much quoted axiom: 'Behind every program and policy is the work of some academic scribbler.' We hark back to concepts and formulations that provide a foundation for action. Alfred North Whitehead wrote that all philosophy is a footnote to Plato.

However if poets are the true legislators of mankind, policy-makers and bureaucrats are the implementers. It is surprising that so little has been written about the leaders and *dramatis personae* in the quest for arms control. Yet as any dedicated newspaper reader knows, individuals do make a difference. At least until oral histories change the prevailing perceptions, the battleground in the Reagan administration over arms control has seemed to pit Secretary of State George Shultz, Ambassador Paul Nitze and Ambassador Max Kampelman among others against Secretary of Defense Caspar Weinberger and Richard Perle. Shultz and his allies favored a continuing dialogue with the Soviets while Weinberger and Perle resented almost every effort at arms control, substituting the view that the United States was capable of prevailing in a limited nuclear conflict. When the INF (Intermediate Nuclear Forces) negotiations finally led to an agreement signed by President Reagan and General Secretary Gorbachev, Weinberger and Perle, whether or not they had planned to leave regardless of the treaty, left the government as the next negotiations were completed.

In every period of American foreign policy, the members of the current administration have ranged themselves in groups, some strongly favoring arms limitations and arms reductions and others opposing serious and single-minded negotiations. The public in turn tends to rally behind those who espouse their views or array themselves against those who are seen as opposing their viewpoint. The same is true of pundits and columnists writing on the subject. Thus columnists like George Will who question the value of almost any negotiations on arms agreements were critical of Shultz while James Reston was sympathetic.

It would seem indisputable, therefore, that individuals matter in arms control as in politics. Studies that illuminate the views of different presidents or leaders are, therefore, important. In most cases, they provide us with lessons on the formulation of arms control policies and with history's manner of dealing with such policies. Were they vindicated or refuted by history and what do historians say in accounting for the consequences and results? What is history's judgment of efforts at arms control or disarmament and what can we learn from that judgment?

If individuals count in whatever assessment is made of arms control, the same must be true as we view negotiators of other nations. Historically, European diplomacy offers examples of skillful and far-seeing diplomats in other countries: Castlereagh and Canning for the United Kingdom, Paul and Jules Cambon for the French, Metternich in Austria and Bismarck for Prussia. In the 1980s, Americans ask what can we say about Soviet negotiators. What about Gorbachev's approach and that of Soviet arms negotiators in Geneva?

Finally, the question of the most appropriate institutions invites consideration. It should be obvious that Soviet and American arms negotiators in Geneva have engaged in a process of long and painstaking discussions. The Soviet and American foreign ministers have played a crucial and decisive role. However, the question also is asked about the institutional arrangements and participants within each of the foreign ministries. Who are the players and what are the resources in knowledge and background on which they can draw? What should be the role of the Defense Department and the military in each country? To invoke public administration language, should they be on tap or on top? What about the Congress? What are its resources and should its participation be elevated in importance in the nuclear age?

To raise the question of institutions is also to suggest that both bilateral and multilateral concerns inevitably come into play? Is arms control a matter for the United Nations? If the arms race is the concern of all 160 member nations, how are the representatives of 160 nations to negotiate on arms and defense issues that are seen primarily as security issues by the superpowers and nuclear states?

To these questions, the contributors to the present volume address their best thoughts and recommendations.

Introduction

Given the vital importance of arms control, it would seem reasonable that scholars and journalists would be addressing themselves to the policies and approaches of successive postwar presidents. Actually, the number of such studies is quite limited. A notable exception is a young political scientist at Widener University in Pennsylvania. He is one of the few researchers who have studied military preparedness and arms control in successive postwar administrations. He is attempting a comprehensive review of defense and arms control policies from president to president. Martin Goldstein came to Virginia to share his earlier findings, especially on Truman and Eisenhower, with the Miller Center family.

Ralph Earle prepared himself for the theory and practice of arms control through long and high-level public service. He was deputy assistant secretary for international security affairs in the Defense Department, a key security and defense position that prepared him well for his role in SALT II. He spent six years in Europe working on defense issues with Defense Secretary Melvin Laird. As a major negotiator of SALT II, he not only put his broad knowledge of defense to use but he gained first-hand knowledge of Soviet approaches to negotiating arms control. His essay is focused both explicitly and implicitly on the subject of negotiating arms control with the Russians.

W. Andrew Banks is a young scholar at the University of Virginia who is a graduate of Wake Forrest. He is especially concerned in his research with Western Europe. His writings fall in the area of American and Soviet foreign policy and he is uniquely qualified to analyze NSC-68, the most important statement of an aggressive strategic view of American responsibilities in the world. In a remarkably objective and detached evaluation of NSC-68, Banks examines its assumptions and the forces and personalities which brought it into being.

We know all too little about the people who are involved in approaches to arms control. Who are the *dramatis personae*, what are their politics and how confident can we be that they will carry out the awesome responsibility of protecting national security while limiting the arms race? Studies such as Banks' and Goldstein's help to supply this information.

William Epstein is the doyen of participant-observers writing on the role of the United Nations in arms control. For more than forty years he has been a leading figure in United Nations efforts at disarmament and arms control. It would be difficult to find any living person who had a more direct knowledge of the United Nations' record and prospects for the future. A Canadian, Epstein has succeeded in maintaining an independent and detached view of the arms control policies of the two superpowers. That lends credence to some of his provisional judgments of Gorbachev's arms control policies, even though history will provide a more enduring judgment. The fundamental question that no one can answer fully is how will the United Nation's balance its advantages and disadvantages in this important sphere and what can it contribute to arms control. Its universal character makes it an appropriate arbiter over what is a global problem. However, does the overrepresentation of the smaller powers in the U.N. and its recurrent decline as a forum for negotiation ("the tower of Babel" criticism) disqualify it as an institution for significant arms agreements among the nuclear powers? Epstein helps us to weigh these considerations.

CHAPTER ONE

The Role of Presidents:
Arms Control and Military Preparedness
From Truman to Reagan

MARTIN E. GOLDSTEIN

NARRATOR: It is a pleasure to welcome Professor Martin Goldstein who is professor of political science at Widener University. He did his undergraduate work at Cornell, his doctoral work at the University of Pennsylvania, and was a protege of a man named Norman Palmer, a great figure in the teaching of international relations.

Martin Goldstein is one of the very few people who has studied military preparedness and arms control in successive postwar administrations. A pattern seems to have been set in that observers report on what Reagan, Carter or Ford are doing or not doing without providing a comprehensive review of policies from president to president. Since there is a paucity of such literature, we invited Martin Goldstein, when we heard of his project, to participate in our arms control series. Among his writings are an important book on *American Policy Toward Laos*, *Nuclear Proliferation: International Politics in a Multinuclear World*, and recently, *An Introduction to America's Foreign Policy: Decision or Drift*.

Professor Goldstein has served as assistant to the deputy director for negotiations and arms control in the Department of Defense, writing policy papers and serving on interagency policy-making committees. He has been a member of the American delegation to the First Preparatory Conference for the United Nations General Assembly Special

Session on Disarmament. He has been chosen for teaching awards, most recently the Christian and Mary Lindback Award for Distinguished Teaching in 1985. Earlier he had been named Outstanding Educator of America for his teaching activities. Professor Goldstein has asked me to remind you that the study is in mid-passage and that findings are becoming clearer as he proceeds. He has completed research on Truman and Eisenhower. For the subsequent presidents, he is still doing his research.

PROFESSOR GOLDSTEIN: I had a most interesting and pleasant day yesterday visiting Monticello, where a couple of things struck me. One was a mirror at the entrance in which you see yourself upside down; another was the placement of the two statues—Thomas Jefferson and Alexander Hamilton opposite each other. As they were rivals in political life, so their busts are now glaring at each other at the front of the building. These sights have a bearing on my investigation. There are two ways of achieving national security and there is a need to balance them. The first position holds that national security can be obtained through military preparedness and the other position puts faith in arms control.

I think most people would agree that the cardinal objective of foreign policy is to protect national security, to make sure that no one invades the country. Traditionally the prime instrument for doing that has been military preparedness—the building of more weapons, the training of more soldiers, and the increase of troops. In the minds of a lot of people, arms control, which used to be called disarmament, is viewed as the opposite of military preparedness. Arms control was thought feasible only when there was a very harmonious international environment and when there was no external threat. It was only certain fuzzy-headed idealists who would think about arms control anyway, and they were dismissed by hard-headed political thinkers.

I'm looking at arms control not as the opposite of military preparedness, or as an alternative to national security, but as a way, along with military preparedness, to enhance national security. As with those two statues and the mirror, there are two sides to reality and two ways to ensure national security. They can both be used at the same time.

There is even a more aggressive way to use arms control and that is to disarm the other side. I'm reminded of a fable by the philosopher, Salvadore de Madariaga. In it a convocation of wild animals takes place. They are concerned about the bad press they are getting; everyone talks about the law of the jungle, with one species always eating another. So these animals, assembled in a stable, begin to talk about arms control. The bear says, "Let's eliminate all weapons except the hug." The eagle says, "Oh, we should do away with everything except talons," and the lion says, "We'll abolish everything but claws." Self-serving attitudes can also apply to states, and they have from time to time. One country may want an arms control agreement that appears to be equitable at first glance, but actually disarms the other side. I'm going to make mention of a couple of those.

The overall framework for my study, then, is to look at national security from two perspectives: that of military preparedness and that of arms control, and examine how each president from Truman to Reagan has dealt with it. As Dr. Thompson has said, I've done some sustained research on the Truman and Eisenhower eras, but not on the others. I shall make some tentative remarks about those other administrations, and try to bring it up to date in looking at the talks that are starting between the Soviet Union and the United States right now.

Let me begin with President Truman. It is clear that his first priority was to win World War II. Once that was done, he turned to the establishment of a new order at home and abroad. Domestically there were three factors that influenced his choice between military preparedness and arms control. One was a balanced budget. Back then the country was not used to living on credit, and there was an enormous war debt. Senator Robert Taft of Ohio took the lead in calling for a balanced budget. This seemed reasonable because there was no apparent threat facing the United States from the rest of the world, which lay in ruins. One way to reduce government spending was to cut back on military spending and we set out to do this. There was a very rapid demobilization reducing the armed forces from eleven and a half million men to two million men by early 1947. The decision to balance the budget was one force acting on Truman in making a choice between military preparedness and arms control.

Another factor was Henry Wallace and the influence of the Progressives. Wallace, then secretary of commerce, was calling for cordial relations with the Soviet Union, halting atomic tests, and implementing New Deal programs at home and abroad. He attributed Soviet aggressiveness to American belligerence, suggesting that "if we were less belligerent, the Russians would be likewise." In answering Wallace, Truman was led toward the advocacy of less military spending.

Next there was a Republican landslide in the congressional elections. The Republicans favored policies that conflicted with a policy of military preparedness. They wanted a balanced budget while also tending toward isolationism in world affairs. A reduced involvement in world affairs would call for a contraction of our armed forces. Domestic forces therefore led Truman away from military preparedness toward reducing arms. But the international context exercised an influence in the opposite direction. Certainly we must consider actions of other states as being as much of a wellspring of foreign policy as domestic events.

There seemed to be a pattern of Communist aggression. Stalin annexed eastern Poland, installed a Communist government in power in Poland, and outmaneuvered an exiled Polish government based in London which was more democratic in orientation. Elections that were supposed to take place in Eastern Europe, as prescribed by the Yalta conference, never took place. At the same time, the Communists had renewed the civil war in China, and in Iran they tried to set up a puppet government in Azerbaijan. So Truman had to contend with these conflicting demands: the domestic ones seemed to lead him toward arms reductions while the international ones seemed to require him to increase military spending.

At first Truman responded more to the domestic pressures; that is, he seemed to lean towards ensuring security through arms limitation rather than buildup. In October of 1945, he delivered a special message to Congress on atomic energy and made the following prescient remarks: "Never in history has society been confronted with a power so full of potential danger and at the same time so full of promise for the future of man, and for the peace of the world." He then went on to call for the creation of a domestic agency directing atomic energy matters with peaceful as well as military application. These were the birth pangs of the Atomic Energy Commission.

Truman called on the international community to come up with arrangements that would result in the universal renunciation of atomic weapons and collaboration on the peaceful use of the atom. Two developments resulted from this: one was a United Nations Atomic Energy Commission, which no longer exists, and the other was the Bernard Baruch proposal. The Baruch proposal was presented to the new United Nations Atomic Energy Commission in June of 1946 by our representative, Bernard Baruch. It was the first major initiative by President Truman to attain postwar security through a non-military preparedness approach. The proposal would create a new international agency under the control of the United Nations to coordinate worldwide atomic energy activity. The United States would turn over its atomic knowledge to this new agency and the agency would disseminate information about peaceful uses of the atom to other countries as well as monitor research around the world. The Baruch proposal included a provision for a system of worldwide controls to insure against cheating. With all of the provisions in place, the United States would dismantle its own nuclear stockpile which at that time consisted of nine bombs. We thought this was a singularly generous proposal. The U.S. was going to forsake its atomic monopoly and share its hard-won atomic knowledge with the whole world.

The Russians didn't quite see it the same way. They distrusted any agency under the United Nations because they distrusted the United Nations itself. At that time it was clearly dominated by the West, and the Soviets would use their veto frequently. The reason the Soviets so often employed the veto was that the Security Council was stacked against them. Any U.N. initiative was therefore something the Russians looked at with a lot of suspicion. At that time they equated international inspection with espionage, as they still do. There is also evidence that they wanted their own atomic arsenal. If you accept the arguments of the likes of Arthur Schlesinger, Jr., that Stalin was paranoid, you may understand why he wanted his own atomic weapons no matter what.

The Russian fear was not entirely unfounded. Suppose this whole Baruch scheme broke down after several years. It was an unprecedented thing to set up a commission to control atomic matters under a new world organization. It was a major undertaking. If the whole thing came apart, where would we be and where would the Russians be? We'd still have our atomic knowledge and our stockpiles—maybe by then we would have even built a few more bombs—and the Russians would have nothing. So they said "nyet," and the Baruch proposal didn't fly.

I sometimes wonder what would have happened if the Baruch proposal had been accepted. It seems to me that it marked one of those junctures in history when things could have taken a different course. Could the nuclear arms race have been headed off? Might it have left the Russians in a position to dominate Europe because of their enormous superiority in manpower? Until this day they are way ahead in conventional forces in Europe. Maybe it would not have been such a good idea. It seems to me that is a question worth asking though. It is sort of fun to speculate about. What would have happened if the Baruch Plan had been accepted?

I think it is interesting to note, though, that Truman's first major initiative to secure American national security was in the arms control area. While all these Baruch proposal debates were going on, the global situation was deteriorating. The communists were starting a civil war in Greece. The Russians were also making a bid to share defense of the Dardanelles with Turkey, which could have led to the domination of Turkey. In February of 1946 Stalin gave a speech in which he said that the wartime cooperation between the socialist world and the capitalist/democratic world was temporary and now that the war was over, this cooperation had to end. The socialist world had to press its advantage. This seemed to signal a major effort to expand communist influence. Shortly thereafter, in March 1947, Truman gave the famous speech that became known as the Truman Doctrine. He asked Congress for military aid to Greece and Turkey, which effectively stemmed the communist threat there.

The Truman Doctrine was clearly a turning point in American foreign policy. It marked a movement away from the attempt to limit arms and cooperate with the Soviets, as represented by the Baruch proposal, and toward military preparedness and confrontation. This was the beginning of containment, and thereafter the Truman administration placed little faith in arms limitation as a way of protecting our national security. Truman began to implement containment in a very serious way with the Marshall Plan, the formation of NATO, and foreign assistance programs, as well as in sending American troops to Korea.

There was one last try for arms control in the Truman administration in November of 1951. We joined with the French and the British in proposing a comprehensive arms control agreement. This agreement would, first of all, call on all members of the U.N. to provide data on the amount of troops and weapons everyone had; there was a lot of dispute as to who had what. Then there would be agreements on limiting and decreasing arms, abolishing atomic weapons, and providing for compliance. Nothing came out of this, because by this time the Cold War was in full swing.

Although this initiative failed to advance the control of arms, it was viewed as a success by Secretary of State Dean Acheson. In his memoirs he wrote, "No doubt existed any longer who stood where or for what. We won a big victory here; this was important because it was good propaganda for us." This became another way to look at arms control, to make the other side look bad. Ever since, propaganda has been a major feature of arms control proposals, and in some cases propaganda seems to have been the main purpose of proposals. That's clearly using arms control for offensive purposes. No longer are we talking about the fuzzy-headed idealists who were thinking about making a better world. Many of those who were now advocating arms control were using it as a bludgeon, and this was one example.

In fact, there came about a curious alliance, which I think still exists, between those who are for arms control and those who are against it. The arms control advocates favor the most far-reaching kinds of arms control proposals. The greatest foes of arms control are usually pushing for the same kinds of proposals, knowing the Russians will never accept them, but giving us the opportunity to look good. We can point to the Russians and say, "It is their fault that a weapons-free world has not come about."

To sum up, the Truman administration, like all others, was concerned about national security. At the end of World War II domestic pressures led Truman to think about limiting arms, but international pressures made him turn to military preparedness. There was a reassessment around 1947 associated with the Truman Doctrine, triggered by George F. Kennan's famous "X" article about containment, and from that point Truman relied more on military preparedness than on arms control.

That brings us to the 1952 election. In that election the Republicans came down hard on Truman's foreign policy. They said it was reactive, and that it offered no hope of a victory over communism. Containment would stop communist expansion, but it wouldn't eliminate communism. The Republicans therefore pledged to "roll back" and overcome communism, not just halt it. This foreign policy line probably won some votes for the Republicans, but it was clearly not the only issue.

Eisenhower came to office, and unlike the present GOP incumbent [Reagan], he was strongly opposed to deficit spending. He said, "You need an adequate defense, but every dollar we spend on arms above what is adequate has a long-term weakening effect upon the nation and its security." Eisenhower felt that excessive government spending was nearly as damaging as a military defeat, and he acted accordingly. One target for cuts was the military, yet the world seemed pretty hostile. So Eisenhower was faced with a choice: to negotiate mutual arms reductions, or to restructure military spending to get more bang for the buck. As we know, he chose the latter course. This was called the "New Look," and it relied heavily on the Strategic Air Command and atomic bombs, instead of the army. Is it not ironic that Eisenhower, the great army general, trimmed down the Army substantially? And it was Eisenhower who came up with the phrase, "military industrial complex," which implies a strong criticism of the military apparatus.

The "New Look" relied on massive retaliation; that is, we would strike the Russian and/or Chinese heartland in retaliation for any aggression anywhere, instead of doing what we had done in Korea, which was to meet aggression where it took place. Massive retaliation required fewer soldiers and a smaller quantity of weapons than Truman's military strategy. Thus Eisenhower was able to reduce military spending from a level of $50 billion to $34 billion by 1955. Military budgets are nearly ten times that high today, but then of course everything seems to cost ten times as much.

In terms of choosing between military preparedness and arms control, there is some resemblance between the Eisenhower administration and the Truman administration. Both viewed the Soviet Union as expansionist. Both placed more reliance on military preparedness than on arms control. But there was certainly a difference in the mix of weapons that they procured. Truman relied on conventional forces as well as atomic forces; Eisenhower relied much more heavily on atomic forces, the reason being his desire to cut military spending.

From reading memoirs, I get the sense that Eisenhower yearned in his heart for arms control. He thought the world needed it. In the Eisenhower years atomic bombs were getting bigger, more destructive, and more numerous. The Soviets were building them too, and it looked as though it would only be a matter of time until more countries would have them. I detect a certain sense of despair in Eisenhower's writings about our failure to bring about arms control, whereas I don't in Truman's memoirs.

As I have noted, Eisenhower decided to rely to a great degree on military preparedness. More tactical nuclear weapons were constructed at that time, and bombs began to give way to missiles. After 1957, when the Russians launched Sputnik, we began to build ICBMs; the Atlas, the Titan, the Minuteman, and the Polaris missiles were deployed, as well as the B52 and B47 bombers. There was a significant atomic military buildup in the Eisenhower years, but there was a lot of arms control activity, too, much more than in the Truman years.

Eisenhower revealed his interest in arms control by appointing a special assistant for disarmament. This was the perennial presidential candidate, Harold Stassen. Eisenhower wouldn't have created this new post in the executive branch if he hadn't been serious about arms control.

In 1953 Eisenhower floated the Atoms for Peace plan. This proposal called on various countries to divert some fissile material to the United Nations for peaceful purposes. One result of the plan was the creation of the International Atomic Energy Agency, which is still functioning under the United Nations today. Again the Russians didn't want to have very much to do with this. It is sometimes said that there was an aggressive element to this idea despite its peaceful sounding name. The Soviets possessed little fissile material at the time. If they gave some to the U.N., they would have little left for constructing weapons.

Another arms control effort was known as Open Skies. Eisenhower proposed that we exchange military blueprints with the Soviets and allow aerial inspection of military facilities. The motivation behind this initiative was the fear of a surprise attack. If either side managed a successful nuclear surprise attack, it might indeed be able to win a war. In a crisis there would then be a great premium on striking first. If you know the other side is thinking in those terms, you begin to think in those terms; if the other side also suspects you are thinking in the terms of a surprise attack, you get a very dangerous spiral of suspicion. This could be prevented if we could constantly inspect Russian military facilities from the sky, and vice versa. But the Soviets refused to allow aerial inspection and admit personnel to the Soviet Union. I think the Russians actually made a mistake here because very shortly thereafter we achieved aerial surveillance of the U.S.S.R. through U-2 flights. The Russians didn't gain the capacity for aerial inspection until satellites came along. With satellites, both sides have open skies now.

In the Eisenhower administration there was also a great deal of negotiation over a nuclear test ban. This topic dominated the arms control agenda for the last half of his administration, though an agreement was never completed. It seemed that we were always out of phase with the Russians; that is, we would complete a series of tests which would put us ahead of the Russians and then we would call for a mutual test ban. Again this was using arms control in a fairly aggressive way, in that we thought of it as a tool to freeze our military superiority, not to build a better world. I certainly don't oppose the creation of a better world, and I think arms control can move us in that direction. But I think arms control has gotten a bad reputation as the prerogative of idealists who don't know what is going on in the world. To return to nuclear testing, we and the Russians were always out of phase. Each called for a test moratorium just when the other side felt a need to gear up for more tests. Extensive negotiations nevertheless were conducted on this subject.

The only ratified arms control agreement during the Eisenhower years came with the Antarctic Treaty of 1959, in which about a dozen countries agreed not to militarize Antarctica. This agreement continues to hold up.

Looking back on the Eisenhower administration, we see that Eisenhower, like Truman, relied more on military preparedness than arms control to bring about national security. Yet there was clearly a much more active arms control agenda under Eisenhower than under Truman. The achievements were slight though. Indeed, the "New Look" with its emphasis on nuclear weapons didn't leave us a whole lot to bargain with. We had already unilaterally dismantled a lot of our military forces because under the doctrine of massive retaliation we wouldn't need a large quantity of infantry and their attendant weapons. A small number of bombers and missiles could do the job.

The Kennedy administration began with a clear emphasis on military preparedness, but there was a marked difference in the way Kennedy allocated our military resources compared to Eisenhower. A Harvard professor by the name of Henry Kissinger had written a book called *The Necessity for Choice* in which he said that we need more than a choice between an atomic response and doing nothing. Kennedy and those around him were persuaded by this argument and felt that there was a need for a wide range of military responses. Kennedy increased the number of combat-ready divisions from eleven to sixteen; he started the Green Berets; he improved our airlift capabilities; and he sent 16,000 military advisers to Vietnam. He was thinking not so much along the lines of "more bang for the buck," but wanted more bangs all around, which cost more bucks, too. Consequently, there was a great increase in military spending under Kennedy.

In 1962 the Cuban missile crisis brought us to the edge of the nuclear abyss. We were eyeball-to-eyeball with the Soviets and the Soviets blinked, as Dean Rusk put it. Afterwards there seemed to be a visceral realization in both the Kremlin and in Washington that the U.S.-Soviet collision course could indeed end up with a fatal crash. It is a little bit like training in the military. In Air Force training we had to crawl under barbed wire and scale some cliffs. One day they started popping off live ammunition. Well, that really gets you to concentrate hard. When they told you to keep your head down, you listened. We were filled with fear. I think we had the same kind of realization after the Cuban missile crisis. It had almost come to the firing of live ammunition, and now there was a new resolve to leaven the U.S.-Soviet rivalry with arms control.

Kennedy and Khrushchev succeeded in bringing about some arms control measures. The hot line was installed and the Limited Test Ban Treaty signed, which prohibits nuclear testing except underground. The Treaty is a disappointment because it has become more of an environmental treaty than a measure for preventing the development of new nuclear weapons, which was its prime purpose.

Moving on to the Nixon-Ford years, I think it is a little ironic that Nixon might be remembered more for arms control than for military preparedness. In 1969 the country was weary of Vietnam, and Nixon gave a speech at Guam which his supporters referred to as the "Nixon Doctrine" and his detractors called the "Guam Doctrine". He said that from then on the United States was not going to Americanize future Third World conflicts. Other countries would have to do the fighting. We would give them aid, but we wouldn't send troops. To me, that represents a retreat from military preparedness, although it does not spell the end of containment.

The ABM Treaty was negotiated during the Nixon years. Both sides agreed to refrain from the employment of the new technology in this Treaty, which I think is being renegotiated to death by President Reagan. The ABM Treaty was a part of the SALT I agreement that put a ceiling on the number of strategic weapons each nation could deploy. Clearly, that's in the arms control category, not military preparedness.

During Nixon's presidency, negotiations also began on reducing the number of ground forces in Eastern Europe and Western Europe in the so-called Mutual and Balanced Force Reduction (MBFR) talks. Little progress has been made. The talks began in 1973, but we and the Russians have yet to agree on how many troops we have in Europe, let alone how to go about reducing them. But for analytical purposes, these negotiations represent a movement toward arms control, not military preparedness.

Let us turn to the Carter presidency, which I sometimes think of as the "schizophrenic presidency" because it seemed to follow two separate and distinct foreign policy approaches in turn. The first part of the presidency ended and the second one began in December 1979 when the Russians invaded Afghanistan. During the "first" Carter presidency, the influence of Secretary of State Cyrus Vance was prevalent. We heard a lot of talk about human rights, the need to cooperate with the Soviets and to get away from an obsession with the Soviet arms build-up. The emphasis was on arms control. After the Russians moved into Afghanistan, Brzezinski's influence as the national security adviser became dominant, and we returned to a Henry Kissinger type of power politics. There was an increase of belligerence toward the Soviets, more denunciation of human rights violations, and a tilt toward military preparedness.

Let me elaborate a little on these two different foreign policies under Carter. The first put a high priority on arms control. We engaged the Soviets in a variety of arms control discussions. For example, there were talks on chemical weapons and on reducing arms in the Indian Ocean area, in which tension has increased somewhat recently. There were the SALT II negotiations, as well as negotiations to limit military incidents at sea where, during training exercises, one of our ships had nudged a Soviet ship and vice versa, an occurrence which could have had serious consequences. The two parties considered a comprehensive test ban and held discussions on a treaty to limit peaceful nuclear explosions such as might be used for dredging canals, building harbors, or moving mountains to extend highways. There were even talks about prohibiting hostile environmental modifications, such as causing rain to fall over another country for an extended period of time. The elimination of anti-satellite satellites, or ASATs, was also considered.

Most of these negotiations came to an end during the second Carter administration. The President withdrew the SALT Treaty from the Senate, created the rapid deployment force, and approved what has become known as the countervailing strategy, which concentrates U.S. forces on the destruction of Soviet war-fighting capabilities, i.e., the equipment the Russians would use during a war. The nuclear weapons required for this purpose would need to be very accurate because they would be aimed at command and control centers and communication hubs. Thus, in the latter part of the Carter administration the emphasis shifted from arms control to military preparedness, a trend that has continued during the current administration and led to the largest peacetime military buildup in American history.

As a result, a multiplicity of new weapons have gone into production, such as the MX missile, the B1 bomber, the Stealth bomber, and the Trident submarine. We have deployed other weapons: the Pershing II and cruise missiles in Europe, for example, which might be taken out very soon, but are still there at the moment. We've also built a six-hundred-ship Navy, and we are about to resume production of chemical weapons. President Reagan is pushing ahead on SDI as well.

Reagan has never been very enthusiastic about arms control. It took him two years to formulate a new SALT position, which I think indicates that it was not one of his highest priorities. Instead, there has been a pretty unambiguous emphasis on military preparedness. The posture of the Reagan administration most closely resembles that of the Truman administration, less so that of the Eisenhower administration, although there are similarities with the latter as well.

My formal thoughts end here for the time being while

I hope that future research will enable me to refine some of these ideas and reach definitive conclusions.

NARRATOR: We now have time for a few questions.

QUESTION: I would like to say a few things about arms control. Admittedly, warfare is immoral as well as ineffective, expensive in a material sense and very cruel. But given human nature, any serious difference of opinion is going to be resolved by force if everything else fails. All you have to do is look around the world today to realize that.

What we have to do over the long run is to eliminate warfare as a means of resolving differences. And that I'm confident we will be able to do maybe four or five thousand years from now. It is unfortunate, but the only reasonable way to protect yourself seems to me to be mutual deterrence.

PROFESSOR GOLDSTEIN: That is probably why there have been so few arms control successes, although there are some twelve to fifteen agreements in force that are respected. Your comment certainly goes to the heart of the issue. I would suggest that in the nuclear age deterrence isn't as comforting as it might once have been. Deterrence, if it should break down, could leave the planet a smoking cinder. Therefore, it might be in the mutual interest of countries to avoid the sort of unrestrained military activity we've seen before the advent of nuclear weapons when there were still winners and losers.

I suspect the reason war has been around so long is that it does solve things. It makes a difference, especially if you are the winner. With nuclear war, that may not be the case. I think there is a growing realization that sometimes an agreement, while not putting you at an advantage, can make the situation safer. For example, agreements that put limits on weapons that you now have don't change the military balance, but don't make you any worse off either. Maybe that's the first step in the journey which you said may last for four or five thousand years. I hope it won't take that long because, if it does, I don't think we will ever get there. Statistically speaking, deterrence is bound to break down sooner or later, either through miscalculation, accident, or lunacy. When I think of certain leaders, Khomeini or Gadhafi, for example, acquiring nuclear weapons, I shudder, because I think that the world might come to an end then.

It is not inconceivable that this might happen because the technology is out in the public domain. Not too long ago, a senior at Princeton published a paper designing a nuclear weapon. It was a term paper based on nonclassified information. When the Pentagon heard about it, it immediately classified it. It's not just the U.S. and the Soviet Union any more who possess nuclear weapons. They are going to be increasingly available to the rest of the world. That's why I feel a certain urgency about trying to stop proliferation and pursue arms control. There is a rational reason for doing so because the alternatives are just unthinkable.

I hope I've responded to your question, although I suspect I haven't.

COMMENT: Not quite. I agree with some of what you said, but war has been around a long time. Maybe Mr. Malthus was right when he said that these days we need a good war because we've got too many people on earth. But I still think in the last analysis war is as inevitable as death. You can try to prolong life, but you are not going to do away with death. In other words, if warfare is inevitable, which it has seemed to be for a long time, and the purpose is to eliminate the other guy, how can you have rules? That's all I'm asking. It has been said that all is fair in love and war. I don't see how you can have rules when the objective is to destroy the other guy.

PROFESSOR GOLDSTEIN: Haven't there been some rules in fighting limited wars, for example?

COMMENT: To a limited extent, yes. We did limit the use of chemical weapons in World War II, quite true, but each side had them.

PROFESSOR GOLDSTEIN: I was thinking of certain rules we followed in Vietnam; for example, we did not use nuclear weapons, and for a long time we did not bomb population centers. I think we followed rules, although I'm not sure the other side did. In Korea, too, we could have done a good bit more with atomic weapons, but we elected not to do so. I do think conflict is inevitable, but I'm not sure that warfare is. And in my opinion one can also talk about arms control without eliminating all arms. With 50,000 atomic weapons in the world, even if you cut them by 25 percent, you still have a lot. While more reductions would be desirable, total elimination is probably impossible because there probably will always be conflict, for which a nation needs to be prepared, to a certain extent. Nevertheless, major cutbacks would be a great comfort to me.

QUESTION: On the matter just under discussion, doesn't the problem come down to what kind of risk people are willing to take? If they insist on guarantees for security, they will be disappointed because they simply aren't out there. The change in the nature of warfare is such that you need to be aware of the presence of risk. Therefore, one should ask what kinds of risks do people subscribe to, or are at least willing to consider?

COMMENT: Another factor you have to look at is politics. A lot of decision-makers are short-range people; they are concerned with what kind of defense contracts they can get for their constituency before the election next year rather than with long-range views about the nature of warfare. If they can bring home a 20, 50, or 200 million dollar contract to their constituency, that gets them a lot of votes. That has to be dealt with too, I think, and not just the economics of a balanced budget.

PROFESSOR GOLDSTEIN: I sometimes wonder what kind of government is in a better position to think about arms control. Democracies seem not to be well suited for long-range planning of almost any kind for reasons you pointed out; in Congress especially, but also in the executive branch, officials seek short-range results. A congressperson doesn't get votes by taking actions which will bring about a better world in eighty years. That doesn't excite the electorate. You've got to show quick results, and one of the best ways of doing that is getting a military contract for your district.

On the other hand, a dictatorship may be better able to afford that kind of long-range thinking. A dictator might calculate that he will be in power for 25 years, so he might be willing to suffer the consequences of a bad short-term decision. He can afford long-term plans, and if anybody disagrees, the ruler will have him shot or put in jail. This realization of a democracy's built-in resistance to long-range planning often troubles me. What was the first point you made?

QUESTION: It addressed the problem of risk, and how to deal with it. What are the guarantees for security?

PROFESSOR GOLDSTEIN: I think there is one risk a lot of people have lost sight of, and that is the risk of continuing military buildups. Recall what happens to your vision when you enter a movie theatre after the film has started. At first, all is dark and you can't see anything. But your eyes gradually become accustomed to the dark, as people have become accustomed to a world with a constant risk of nuclear war. No one experiences alarm over the skyrocketing accumulation of weapons. Instead the risks are associated with cutting back weapons. There are hazards in deterrence because statistically there is a good chance it will break down. Perhaps this won't occur for 50, 100 or 250 years. Deterrence must hold forever, though, and I believe this is too much to expect.

Despite the greatest precautions, airplanes crash. All systems malfunction sooner or later and deterrence will too. So to me there is a great risk in continuing the superpower military buildup.

NARRATOR: If totalitarian governments have a certain advantage over democracies, how do we account for Gorbachev's sense of urgency—if he has it—about reforming the economy and cutting back on nuclear weapons?

PROFESSOR GOLDSTEIN: Let's assume that's true. I guess there are a couple of ways you can account for that. One might be that he wants to lead a vital, strong nation and, reflecting Eisenhower's thinking, Gorbachev might conclude that if you spend too much on the military you are taking resources away from other sectors. The Soviet economy is infamous for chronic shortages of consumer goods. They could rectify this by reducing military spending.

Americans may not perceive Gorbachev correctly. We salute him for his good sense, though he might be creating a much more dangerous rival for us by revitalizing the Soviet economy. On the other hand, Gorbachev may simply be acting in a manner which we are not used to, that of a farseeing statesman who is pursuing grander schemes than just winning the next election, or overcoming one's rivals. Perhaps Gorbachev really wants to create a safer, better world and he sees military build-down as a way to do it. It's awfully early though, to tell if that is how he feels. But these are two possible interpretations.

QUESTION: As a follow-up to that, if some of the economists are correct in predicting a serious recession in the early 1990s, what effect will that have on the desire of superpowers to reduce armament?

PROFESSOR GOLDSTEIN: I don't think it will have much of any effect because governments elevate national security factors above sound economics. If we cannot assure the safety of our country, what good is a healthy economy?

If you look at the U.S.A. and Russia, there has been a steady arms buildup since 1945 despite some economic slow-downs. To the people who make these decisions, economics seem to be a lesser factor than national security.

QUESTION: Does it make any difference which party in the United States is in power?

PROFESSOR GOLDSTEIN: Individuals matter more than party. Carter, for example, using the same facts and figures as his predecessor, arrived at a much reduced threat assessment with regard to the U.S.S.R. Clearly, our data on Soviet forces hadn't changed, but the President's perception had. Personalities of leaders may have a big effect on the perception of the threat.

Over time, these perceptions may be strongly influenced by one's role in an organization. I remember when Jimmy Carter started out he wore cardigan sweaters and carried his own brief case. He was behaving like the sweet kid from next door who just happened to get himself elected president. By the end of his presidency, he was wearing blue suits and allowing an aide to carry his briefcase. In short, he was slipping into the "role" we associate with the chief executive.

Have you ever noticed that everyone who becomes secretary of defense eventually advocates more military spending? The point is that government officials gradually adopt behavior patterns associated with their roles. The role of the president is to protect the country. He protects the country by acquiring more weapons. It takes a strong personality, I think, to break out of these roles. Carter wasn't able to; by the end of his administration he had turned into a hawk, rejected negotiations with the U.S.S.R. and begun an arms buildup. Only a mighty personality can shatter and restructure a role, as when Roosevelt rejected laissez-faire and adopted the New Deal.

QUESTION: Couldn't Carter's hawkish stance perhaps be the result of being better informed after having been President for awhile? He was more aware of the dangers in the world and knew them firsthand.

PROFESSOR GOLDSTEIN: Well, it could be. But you are suggesting that there is a basic reality of a hostile world which requires that one should always have more weapons, and every president needs to grow into that awareness.

COMMENT: No, what I mean to say is that if you are well informed day after day, your thinking may change after you have been the president for a couple of years.

PROFESSOR GOLDSTEIN: Maybe so. You could possibly find evidence for that, but I think it also depends upon the people we have as presidents. My students occasionally ask, "Why don't we get better people in the White House?" Not that the ones we've had were all dreadful by any means, but our election system doesn't seem to be capable of bringing forth the best presidents.

COMMENT: The best were before television.

PROFESSOR GOLDSTEIN: I think there is a lot to that. But if we had presidents with a broader vision and greater awareness of the risks of a constant arms buildup, we might have a better chance of avoiding confrontations such as the Cuban missile crisis. We also don't want someone who is too naive and says, "Let's abolish all the weapons. I'm sure the Russians will follow suit and we will all be happy." That's dangerous, too. But in my opinion, we've had a long succession of presidents who lacked a broader vision. It could well be that Gorbachev is one such individual, though it is too early to tell. He may be a statesman who raises his sights above narrow national advantage, thus benefitting the world as a whole.

QUESTION: Is there any concern among your students about the threat of nuclear war?

PROFESSOR GOLDSTEIN: No. There is very little concern. Their primary concern is with what job they will be able to get after college if they major in a particular field.

QUESTION: Why do you think there is that lack of concern?

PROFESSOR GOLDSTEIN: I don't detect much of a concern about nuclear war among the rest of us. I suppose young people pick that up. I cannot think of a movie or television show, for example, that deals with this issue now, and the media reflects to a large extent our current preoccupations.

COMMENT: I've been doing a lot of work on the historical relationship of the military to American society. It seems to me that there is sort of a boom-and-bust cycle, with the military being built up when there is a war and then dismantled after it's over. Might there be a problem arising from these transitions between arms control and military preparedness? If one emphasizes arms control, particularly to the public, then one quickly gets reduced public acceptance for the continuation of any military preparedness. Arms control acts as a sort of flag saying, "we can deemphasize military things now. We are in the arms control phase." From here we easily get into illusions about arms control which then make it hard to spend money on all things military. How do we get out of this dilemma without fundamentally changing American cultural and political attitudes towards war and the military?

PROFESSOR GOLDSTEIN: Maybe we *can* change some of those attitudes. Among Americans there is a tendency to see military preparedness and arms control as opposites, not as two different ways to ensure national security. Perhaps that is a philosophical tradition. It used to be true that you could acquire weapons, fight a war, and scrap them when the war is over. I don't think that is true any more. Maybe education is the answer in making us realize that we need both arms control and military preparedness to survive, and that it's not one instead of the other.

QUESTION: One of the interesting things about the Reagan administration is its emphasis upon military preparedness as a means to achieve arms control, and not as an alternative to achieving security. With regard to the INF agreement, the Reagan administration argues that it has come close to an agreement with the Russians because it was tough and deployed the intermediate range missiles, the Pershing II and cruise missiles, in the face of a lot of flak from the peace movement. Do you think this is a valid argument? That's the first question. The second question is, even if it isn't a valid argument, do you think that if we achieve an INF agreement that the public will finally buy this notion that we need to build up arms to achieve arms control?

PROFESSOR GOLDSTEIN: You'll never be able to prove it's not a valid argument and it may well be. Certainly it is to the conservatives. If there is an INF agreement, conservatives will say, "This is the strategy we have to follow. The Russians understand only toughness and force. If we are tough then we can get a good SALT agreement."

Based on that argument we might expect some major military buildups in the attempt to get the Russians to agree to more arms cuts.

Let us not forget, however, that there are other reasons that have moved the Russians toward arms control agreements: the desire to save money, restructure the economy, and ease away from confrontation.

QUESTION: Do you think the public will buy that argument, that you need to build up first before getting an agreement with the Russians?

PROFESSOR GOLDSTEIN: I don't think it is that much of a watershed. I think that those with a hawkish philosophy will say, "See, I told you so." Those who feel otherwise will say, "Well, let's emphasize the other reasons." It will be very hard to tell whether the public as a whole accepts that argument. The fact that the treaty comes at the end of the Reagan administration, though, may have some effect on the next election. If it had come at the beginning of the administration the republic would have probably forgotten about it, and it wouldn't have made much of an impact. But coming now, I would think it would be a help to the more hawkish-minded candidates who say, "We are going to continue this tradition. We want peace, we want to get rid of arms, but the way to do it is by increasing military spending first." Therefore the treaty could have some bearing on the 1988 election.

COMMENT: I understood you to include the Marshall Plan and Point Four as part of military preparedness, while it seemed to me that the economic aid aspect of those plans was very important. I wondered if you thought that if some of these people with broader vision became influential in our government, they might consider using an economic weapon rather than more missiles.

PROFESSOR GOLDSTEIN: Economic aid is a weapon, and therefore a means of coercion.

COMMENT: We don't use it that way.

PROFESSOR GOLDSTEIN: I think I mentioned it as part of the containment policy of the Soviet Union, but, strictly speaking, I would not equate the Marshall Plan with military preparedness.

COMMENT: I understand that.

PROFESSOR GOLDSTEIN: Let us remember that the motivation for our whole foreign aid program is the desire to contain communism. I don't think we would have a foreign aid program of any proportions if it were not for the Cold War. Before World War II we didn't have an aid program except for flood or famine relief. The reason for the Marshall Plan was clearly to shore up Western Europe's economy because we feared the communists would take over either from within through elections or from without through an advance of the Red Army.

QUESTION: Why don't we have a new Marshall Plan?

PROFESSOR GOLDSTEIN: For one thing, the American public isn't that crazy about the idea. The sum of money we've spent on foreign aid is only explicable in the context of our desire to contain Soviet influence and prevent revolutions which always offer an opportunity for communists to take power. The term "foreign aid" is poor because it suggests disinterestedness. A better term would be "international self-help." Perhaps those words would earn more public support for this sorely needed effort.

QUESTION: How do you evaluate the activities of the World Bank?

PROFESSOR GOLDSTEIN: Even with the World Bank there is an element of self-interest because this country thrives on worldwide stability, and the World Bank helps provide that. We are like a wealthy person who lives in the large mansion on the top of the hill, who supports law and order because he wants to maintain the status quo. In that sense the World Bank also serves our containment purposes, but there is an altruistic motive to it as well, as was true of the Marshall Plan.

NARRATOR: I know I speak for all of you in thanking Professor Goldstein very much.

CHAPTER TWO

Negotiating Arms Control
With the Soviets

AMBASSADOR RALPH EARLE II

NARRATOR: We all remember during the discussions on SALT II listening to people argue the issues pro and con. At the height of the controversy I tuned in on some program and the person who made more sense in explaining SALT II than anybody I had listened to was Ambassador Ralph Earle, II. For six years in Europe, as well as in the Pentagon, he had worked on defense issues. In Europe he worked with Mel Laird, and in the Defense Department he served as deputy assistant secretary for International Security Affairs (ISA). He has dealt with different facets of the defense issue as few Americans have.

He has also served as a member of several law firms and is now associated with the Lawyers Alliance for Nuclear Arms Control. In that capacity, and from his discussion of the whole arms control issue, he brings the same clarity that I remember from the earlier discussion of SALT II.

AMBASSADOR EARLE: I'm honored to be here. I will focus on a few points and then I will be interested in hearing your views and will try to answer any questions that may arise.

Just before we came in, I was talking about my ignorance fifteen years ago of arms control. Life is funny; you end up doing things you never expect to do and certainly my involvement with the issue of arms control was one that I never expected. I have found it rewarding, gratifying, and frustrating and, on balance, if I had it to do all over again, I would. I have dealt with some very interesting people, and I've dealt with some very unpleasant people. The subject matter, however, has remained constantly fascinating to me and is obviously important to all of us.

This is not going to be a particularly cheerful exposition because I am depressed about the status of treaties, ratified and unratified. We have the SALT II treaty. I spent six years negotiating it, but it was never ratified for many reasons. Generally, I think, the best became the enemy of the good. The treaty was attacked for not solving all problems, including the common cold, which in my view was an unfair attack. We never pretended that it did that, or a number of other things. It was, of course, fraught with bad luck; the treaty was plagued by the so-called "discovery" of the brigade in Cuba, the Afghanistan invasion, and a very strong right-wing challenge to the presidency by Governor Reagan. Despite the failed efforts to ratify the treaty, we did agree that the United States would take no steps to undercut it so long as the Soviets behaved similarly.

In May of 1986, the Reagan administration announced that it would no longer adhere to the limits of the SALT II treaty, and in December of that year it exceeded one of the sub-limits of the treaty by deploying one more B-52 equipped with long-range cruise missiles than the treaty allows. I honestly don't know why the administration did that, because to me it was a genuinely mindless act. One more bomber makes absolutely no difference in the strategic equation, and it opens the door for the Soviet Union to exceed the limits with a clear conscience and with a far greater potential to increase their military deployments.

Paul Warnke exaggerates when he says the Soviets turn missiles out like sausages, but they do have open lines for missiles that we do not have. We have just begun to produce the MX, and we are limited to fifty by the Congress. I think moving beyond the treaty limits was a mistake, militarily as well as politically. In my view, it is one more instance in which the international law system under which we operate has been undermined. I hasten to add, however, that the treaty was not binding, so what was done was not illegal. We had a perfect right to abrogate it, or announce its abrogation, but sometimes things that are permitted aren't necessarily wise.

Currently, in the area of treaties the treatment of the ABM Treaty is more important. This leads me into a brief discussion of what I think is a very serious issue. The ABM Treaty was signed in 1972 and, with its protocol in 1974, limited each side to one ABM site. It was ratified by a vote of eighty-eight to two by the United States Senate and thereby became the law of the land under our Constitution. The ABM Treaty is of indefinite duration and it is, clearly, legally binding on us and on the Soviet Union. It has been challenged now by a reinterpretation of the Treaty, conjured up by the legal adviser to the State Department (Judge Abraham Sofaer), which expands what is permitted under it. As Senator Sam Nunn has pointed out, this reinterpretation raises serious constitutional questions. Even if the State Department is right, the fact remains that in 1972 when the Treaty was up for hearings before its ratification, the administration stated unequivocally, in writing, that the Treaty barred testing in space. That statement was in response to a written question by Senator Barry Goldwater. Obviously, the Senate relied on that letter because it was ratified by a vote of eighty-eight to two.

Therefore, I think Senator Nunn was right when he suggested to President Reagan that for this administration to reinterpret the Treaty in a fashion that would permit testing in space and development of space based weapons raises a serious constitutional question. Can one administration, fourteen years after a treaty has been ratified, advise the Senate and take action as if the treaty meant something entirely different from what the administration had told the Senate at the time of its ratification? These are very serious problems, and they should be discussed and debated. Obviously, I have my own views about whether the interpretation or reinterpretation is legally correct, and about what the constitutional concerns of reinterpretation are, given the advice to the Senate at the time of ratification and fourteen years of consistent iterations by both Democratic and Republican administrations. Indeed, the negotiators themselves have said that they meant the original narrow interpretation.

I think these are legal questions; they are constitutional questions, and, hopefully, the administration will take Senator Nunn's advice. He expressed his concern pretty strongly and the administration will have thorough consultation before it takes what I consider an unfortunate, unwise and illegal step. Underlying this discussion, however, is an issue which has hardly been touched on by the press, the media, or by commentators, and that is the reversal that the SDI program represents in terms of basic national security strategy.

If I can go back a few years, in 1967 President Johnson met in an impromptu fashion with Premier Kosygin in Glassboro, New Jersey. At a luncheon there, Secretary McNamara explained to Kosygin that in the nuclear age in which we were then living, with delivery systems that were fast, efficient and, by those day's standards, reasonably accurate, defenses were simply unwise and unreal. Further, although it was not a particularly joyous prospect, the facts were that the nuclear genie was out of the bottle and that we would forever live under the specter of a nuclear destruction.

Kosygin apparently responded quite angrily, and when the Soviets get angry, they tend to talk a lot about morality—or maybe it's the other way around. He responded angrily saying that offensive weapons were immoral because they killed people and defensive weapons were moral because they killed weapons. That, of course, is a very simplistic view, and yet I think one that has been adopted by President Reagan. Ironically, then, the Soviets liked the idea of SDI at that time while we did not.

The SALT negotiations began two years later in 1969. Over the period of time from November 1969 until May of 1972, when the ABM Treaty was signed, the Americans were able to convince the Soviets of the rectitude and propriety of Bob McNamara's position. When the ABM Treaty was signed and ratified, it was, in effect, a tacit agreement between the two sides that deterrence was the best and only way to keep the peace. Whether you wanted to call it deterrence, or if you preferred the pejorative acronym MAD (for "mutual assured destruction"), that was the way we were going to have to live. Unhappy as that may have been, that's the way it was.

If Winston Churchill had had an air defense system in 1941 or 1942 that shot down 90 percent of the Nazi bombers, he would have been very happy because in three days the German bomber command would have been destroyed and he would have lost only several hundred blocks of London.   However, if tomorrow we have a 90 percent effective defense against the 10,000 nuclear warheads, 1,000 warheads will get through.   We won't lose 300 blocks of New York; we would lose New York and 300 other cities.   It is an entirely different ball game now, and I think that is a very basic thing that we have to keep in our minds.

This brings me to the heart of the issue.   For almost forty years we have achieved a level of peace, based on deterrence.   In my view, the Strategic Defense Initiative represents an effort to change that policy—not slightly, not somewhat, but completely.   In President Reagan's words, "the desire to make nuclear weapons obsolete" means that it must be done defensively.   I consider that to be an issue that should be brought to the attention of the American people and before the Congress to be debated thoroughly. We are really nit-picking now, even though I say there is a constitutional issue, but we should not even be discussing the constitutional issue until we determine whether or not a defense is a better way to maintain and enhance the national security of the United States.   I don't think that issue has been addressed anywhere, certainly not to my satisfaction.   I think people are unaware that this represents, or could represent, a dramatic change in our whole national security posture.

Personally, I am an opponent of SDI.   I'm not a scientist, but those scientists whom I respect basically say that it won't work.   Of course, SDI has not yet been defined; we ought to be told what it is supposed to do for us.   Ninety percent effectiveness does not do us any good at all because we would not lose a few blocks of one city, but many whole cities.   In addition, the worst case scenario that I can see for SDI is in the possibility that it works. That may sound odd, but defenses, unilateral defenses particularly, become very offensive.

I am reminded of the movie "Shane" with Jack Palance in his black suit and Alan Ladd in his white hat, both standing in the street ready to shoot at each other. I think if Alan Ladd had jumped behind a stone wall, Jack Palance would not have thought that that was a defensive move; rather he would have found it very threatening. The Soviets see our desire to put up defenses as very threatening and aggressive. Mr. Weinberger has said, and I quote him I think verbatim, "My God, if they got it before we did, it would be as if we had no nuclear weapons." Well, consider what Mr. Weinberger's counterpart in the Kremlin thinks. The Soviets will obviously take steps to insure that they are not put in that defensive position where we can shoot at them yet they cannot shoot at us. That's a terrifying situation for a national leader to be in. Further, if it appears that we are about to gain that position strategic stability will vanish, and the temptation to strike before you are struck will increase.

One subject which I have not addressed, but one which I would be happy to discuss if anybody is interested, is negotiating with the Soviets. I would be happy to address that or any other issue, but I would like to have your comments on what I've said, even though I'm sure not all of you agree with me.

NARRATOR: Thank you very much. I know all of us would like to hear about the Soviets as negotiating partners or adversaries. We can do that now or later, but perhaps we should first see if people have questions on the points you've made.

QUESTION: Do we have any knowledge of what the Soviets are doing on SDI? Assuming that we change our policy and abandon SDI, can we be sure the Soviets will reciprocate?

AMBASSADOR EARLE: They have quite a vigorous research program, as we have had from day one. I am not suggesting that we terminate our research. The thing that troubles me is that we are, in effect, saying "We will break the Treaty by testing in space," while they have made no indication that they would do that. The Treaty permits unlimited testing on the ground in fixed land bases. You can test whatever lasers or exotic x-rays you care to and I think they have progressed in that area as we have. What troubles me about SDI, the initiative part, is that it presumes that if our research is successful we will go on to break the Treaty.

The Soviets have a program, and we have always had a program as they have. We should continue ours, and they will continue theirs. It is moving outside of the Treaty and upsetting the balance which is created by the deterrent posture, which both of us have maintained, that troubles me. I'm glad you asked that question because it gave me a chance to clarify. I have, in fact, encouraged research. We must do it, if for no other reason than to stay with the state of the art and to see what they are doing, because there might be some major breakthrough and we ought to know about that.

QUESTION: When you say we need to conduct research in the area, are you talking about the area of deterrence *per se* or the area of defensive weapons or all areas, the full gamut?

AMBASSADOR EARLE: I'm referring to ballistic missile defense research. Whether we use particle beams, lasers, or kinetic kill vehicles or whatever, we ought to, and we will, expand our knowledge as much as we can about what is possible and what is feasible. I fully expect the Soviets are going to do the same.

QUESTION: But if they are still doing research, at what point does it become an SDI program? How do you make the distinction between research and initiative?

AMBASSADOR EARLE: I simply make the distinction in the terms of the ABM Treaty, which permits each side one site with no more than a hundred launchers or the equivalent, which means that under the Treaty you cannot have a national defense, and if you can only protect one site, it is not worth having at all. People say, "Well, the Soviets have a deployed system around Moscow." It is true that they have something called the "Galosh" system that is based on 1950s technology. The best it could do would be to shoot down a hundred warheads, because it is limited to a hundred launchers. Since we have around 1,000 warheads aimed at Moscow, it doesn't matter.

In the late 1960s and early 1970s we developed an ABM system that was superior to the ones the Soviets still have deployed. We actually completed it and deployed it around Grand Forks Air Force Base. When President Nixon signed the protocol to the Treaty in 1974 that reduced sites from two to one, we said, in effect, it just isn't worth keeping. It is mothballed, and it has been mothballed for fifteen years because we properly concluded that defending one missile site with 1960s technology was not worth the effort.

To come back to your original question, in my view the area I'm referring to is that area which is permitted by the ABM Treaty. As long as we both live within that Treaty, with its primary prohibitions against the testing and development, and clearly the deployment of missile defense systems, we would both be better off.

QUESTION: Ambassador, the Soviets have shown that they are willing to make fairly dramatic concessions in arms control over the last year or eighteen months for which there are at least two alternative explanations. Doves tend to say that it's because of Gorbachev's peaceful inclinations and desire to rebuild his domestic economy. Hawks tend to say it's because of the Reagan military build-up and the threat of SDI. You have had a lot of experience dealing with the Soviets; in your view, which is the more nearly correct? Do they react better to strength or conciliation?

AMBASSADOR EARLE: That's a very good question. Though I have had very few dealings with them in recent years, I can tell you that I did go to a meeting in New York last week at which I listened to both Secretary Vance and Secretary Kissinger talk. They both felt that Soviet domestic priorities were driving Gorbachev's willingness to make concessions. They had spent several hours with him and said that he appeared to be genuinely concerned. He has great programs and plans for the Soviet Union. When asked how he was going to implement them he said quite candidly, "I don't know, but I will try to find a way to get this done." Vance and Kissinger agreed that he is genuinely interested in taking the heat off himself on the foreign affairs issues so that he can concentrate on the domestic ones.

I think that if SDI has a justifiable existence, it has been as an instrument to drive the Soviets to think harder about the major offensive cuts. I do not, however, think that is what got them to the table. In fact, I think it is what drove them away from the table in Reykjavik.

Both Kissinger and Vance believe that there cannot be any deal on offensive weapons until we make major concessions on SDI. I agree with that view. We are clearly technologically ahead, but that doesn't mean that they won't catch up with us. If we reverse the situation, however, let's assume they were technologically ahead, and Gorbachev came to the table and said, "We are going to continue all out on our program to minimize the effect of your missiles, and we want you to cut yours 50 percent." You would walk away from that table very fast.

QUESTION: Do you see any meeting ground on SDI between our position and the Soviet position where this could be resolved?

AMBASSADOR EARLE: Well, again it depends on whom you ask about what it means. I do not think SDI has ever been defined properly. I think the suggestion that the Soviets have made, to live ten years within the narrow interpretation of the ABM Treaty, is a totally satisfactory one. Many people say that unless we do something nutty, and I think deploying a system of kinetic kill vehicles would perhaps be nutty, we really aren't in a position to go beyond that in ten years anyway. In effect, we really would not be giving up anything. I'm surprised that the Soviets are willing to say ten years, because I would be tempted, if I were they, to say, "Damn it, this is of indefinite duration and you have ratified it eighty-eight to two and now you have to live with it for the indefinite duration." Apparently, however, Gorbachev has said "If you promise not to break out for ten years, then we can discuss these other items." There are some who think that we should not do that because a ten year moratorium will always mean a twenty year, a thirty year, and a fifty year moratorium. That's the slippery slope argument. Of course, that is fine with me. I would be happy to see us get on that slippery slope and abide by the Treaty.

QUESTION: Given the disarray in the present administration, do you think there is reasonable chance that any of these proposals are going to get anywhere, as far as working out something with the Soviets while this administration is in office?

AMBASSADOR EARLE: The current disarray is, of course, one factor. Even without the Iran-Contra affair, however, whether this administration—and I use that as a collective noun—really wants arms control is questionable.

Now there is talk that maybe they came so close to a deal in Reykjavik on the reduction of intermediate nuclear forces in Europe that it is possible. My own view is that the Soviets are unlikely to make a partial deal. Four days before we finished the SALT II treaty we still had some issues to button up and the Soviet negotiator said to me, "And I remind you, nothing is agreed until everything is agreed." I may not be 100 percent right on that, because I think it is conceivable that they could make a decision to remove their SS-20s from western Soviet Union if they thought it would be of sufficient political value in western Europe. The situation, of course, is complicated because while we have been debating, and this is one of the frustrations of being a negotiator, the guys in the laboratories and the test areas who are always much quicker forge ahead.

While we've been debating the SS-20 for eight years, they have developed the SS-21, 22, and 23. Although these missiles possess much shorter range, they clearly threaten large portions of western Europe too, or certainly would in a battlefield situation.

These negotiations really come down to the political will of the two leaders. I spent seven years in Geneva before reaching an agreement. Averell Harriman went to Moscow, and he got the Limited Test Ban in three days because they wanted it and we wanted it. You have to have a coming together, a synergism of the two political forces before you have an agreement. The current chances of that sort of union are low, but I would not eliminate the possibility of some kind of agreement.

NARRATOR: If the present administration doesn't get an agreement, what are the prospects for a less conservative administration successfully defending an agreement in the Congress?

AMBASSADOR EARLE: One of the problems that Ronald Reagan could run into on any arms control agreement that he negotiated is Senate ratification. Would Mike Dukakis or even George Bush have an easier time gaining ratification? Jack Kemp could, but could George Bush get an arms agreement ratified? It's a hard question, and that's a subject for another talk. I do think, however, that we ought to amend the Constitution to get away from the two-thirds ratification. The two-thirds ratification was put into the Constitution when the Senate was composed of entirely different kinds of people than it is now, and it is too unfair a burden to put on treaties to ask for a two-thirds vote of approval.

In 1979, even in the best of circumstances, we knew that there were between seventeen and twenty senators who would vote against any treaty with the Soviet Union. That means you have to get seven-eighths rather than two-thirds because those fifteen to twenty people are just eliminated from your consideration. The answer to a successful defense in Congress is a good agreement.

We came up with a good agreement in SALT II. It could have been ratified, even after all those unfortunate events.

NARRATOR: It should not have been withdrawn?

AMBASSADOR EARLE: I don't think so. You are looking over your shoulder at the Senate all the time when you are negotiating a treaty. The ratification requirement can give you some leverage, but once your treaty has been signed, then you have a real problem with getting it ratified.

QUESTION: Several years ago the concept of unilateral nuclear disarmament became quite popular with some groups.

Do you think there is a place for unilateral action in the field of disarmament?

AMBASSADOR EARLE: Logically and militarily there is, politically there is not. That's oversimplified, but Jimmy Carter, as president-elect, had a meeting with the Joint Chiefs of Staff in the Blair House in December before his inauguration, and he asked at that meeting, "How many weapons do we really need to deter the Soviet Union?" At that time we had 7,000 or 8,000, maybe only 6,000 deliverable strategic warheads. He said later that he had in mind about 1,000. Well, the word of that question and discussion leaked and he was very severely criticized for it. Some people were going to criticize anything he did, while others had some military concerns, but the major and most valid concern was that it would be politically unwise.

Suppose that we had unilaterally reduced to 1,000 warheads and the Soviets had kept their 7,000. In the Third World the Soviets could make much of the fact that they were seven times as strong as the United States. That is one possible result of unilateral reduction, even though our 1,000 warheads were just as big a threat to the Soviet Union as their 7,000 were to us. It's all overkill. It's hard for me to imagine, politically, a president or Congress or both embarking on a unilateral reduction. Although it is perfectly sensible, it just won't wash.

QUESTION: What about the question of verification or compliance with treaty limitations?

AMBASSADOR EARLE: I have looked at that very hard. The looser the agreement, the happier the Soviets are, because that permits a unilateral interpretation of vague words. Regardless of whether it is loose or tight, however, they are going to push right up to the very edge. The question later becomes, how close to that edge have they gotten and have they gone over it?

We wrote the Treaty with that question in mind. When I was testifying before the Intelligence Committee Scoop Jackson, who was not any great friend of the Treaty, asked, "Did you pay any attention to verification when you were negotiating?" I took home a copy of the Treaty that night and with a red crayon I crossed out all of the provisions in the Treaty which would have been unnecessary if the other party had been somebody we trusted, like God. I crossed out 95 percent of that Treaty. The operative parts of the Treaty, putting aside verification, were very simple; they were just numbers.

As for compliance, with respect to SALT II, I think the alleged violations are very questionable. I don't think it is a very serious issue except for one serious and clear violation, and that is the radar that they are building in Krasnoyarsk. It's a clear violation of the ABM Treaty, but I don't think it is significant militarily. I do not think it gives them the basis for battle management and continental defense, but it is clearly a violation of the treaty, and they shouldn't be permitted to get away with it.

I did just read, however, that Georgi Arbatov says that they have stopped construction of it. I think it is about 90 percent finished, yet he said they did stop construction. They are obviously conscious of it. On the whole their record has been pretty good. When you consider that they have destroyed over 1,500 of their strategic systems in order to stay within the limits, that's an impressive fact, because they hate to throw anything away. They hang on to Napoleonic war cannons just in case they find that they can use them. You have to watch them all the time, since they will push and push. You have to hammer them. If you hammer them on it privately—not publicly—they will find a face-saving way to comply. This is somewhat of an aberration, but they do some very odd things.

At the end of the SALT II negotiations they had had, for a number of years, eighteen launchers of heavy ICBMs at a test range. We were pretty suspicious that they weren't really test and training launchers. We asked them why they cleared the snow from around those eighteen when it snowed—and none of the other launchers? Why were the roads leading to those launchers always clear of snow? They insisted that they were test and training, so that I thought we were at a real impasse. About three weeks before the end of the negotiations, however, they came in and blithely said, "We are going to destroy twelve of those eighteen test training launchers we have at Tyuratam, and make sure you know the other six are just for test and training. To save face they wouldn't admit that they were operational. They went beyond anything we would have suggested for them to do. So maybe they will destroy Krasnoyarsk in some great fit of honesty; they are sometimes odd to deal with.

I would say on balance that their compliance record is good. Clearly, however, it is not perfect, and you've got to keep after them. When you deal with them rationally and calmly, and not in the newspapers, you are more likely to find them accommodating.

NARRATOR: To what extent did you find that the Soviets simply play the same phonograph record that you had already heard over and over again? And, to what extent did any of the people you dealt with on SALT II have any independence in their negotiating? You did mention that we might come back to the business of negotiation.

AMBASSADOR EARLE: Basically, they were like us in that. They were very constrained by their instructions. One of the problems of negotiating for the United States government on strategic arms is that all the heavyweights in Washington are interested, and thus everybody looks over your shoulder all the time. The Soviets are in the same situation. I think the only real aberration we have seen is the so-called walk in the woods between Paul Nitze and Kvitsinski. I cannot believe, however, that Kvitsinski didn't have instructions to do that. I think Paul Nitze went beyond his instructions, but that's the only time I can think of a U.S. negotiator really going beyond his instructions. I don't think that Kvitsinski did.

Once, a Soviet negotiator cut a deal on Tuesday, and on Wednesday welshed on it, saying, "The military made me change my mind." That is the only time I have ever seen a Soviet negotiator change a position openly and admit why. They are like any group of people and, as I said, some of my own frustrations came from my side of the table.

The thing I found astonishing was that with few exceptions I think the Soviet delegation would have been just as happy working for the Czar. I'm sincere when I say that they are Russians first; the fact that they are part of the Soviet Union is secondary. They are very patriotic and they care a lot, but we never got any speeches about communism. We never engaged ourselves in that sort of activity because they would not have listened. It would have been boring, and they really weren't interested in talking about it anyway.

QUESTION: How did they handle the language barrier?

AMBASSADOR EARLE: Consecutive translation; the languages are very far apart. It made for somewhat stultified dialogue. I would speak three sentences and then my interpreter would say three sentences in Russian and then the response would be similar. Sometimes it caused real problems. The one I remember best was my chief interpreter coming in and saying "We have a real problem with MIRVs." I asked, "Why do you have a problem with MIRVs?" He said, "Well, 'multiple independently targetable reentry vehicle' in verbatim translation from the Russian becomes 'self-dividing front end'." I said, "We must have a better phrase than that," and he said, "I can make up a better phase, but that's what their military calls it; therefore, that's what it is."

At the end there were four copies of the treaty: two in English, two in Russian. The reason there were two of each was because one begins "the United States of America and the Union of Soviet Socialist Republics" and the other begins "the Union of Soviet Socialist Republics." We also changed the signature blocks at the end for Brezhnev and Carter; they were reversed. The interpreters, both Soviet and American, all had to get together and agree that both versions meant the same thing in each language. In fact the treaty says that in both languages each one is of equal force and effect. More of the Soviets spoke more English than we did Russian. On the other hand, our interpreters were much better than their interpreters because all of our interpreters had been born in Russia, and none of their interpreters had been born in the United States. Overall, I don't think language disability constituted a problem. It made things a little slower, but I don't think it was a major problem for us.

QUESTION: Some of their negotiators spoke English though, didn't they?

AMBASSADOR EARLE: Their chief negotiator, Victor Karpov, spoke better English than any of their interpreters. Many of them had served in the embassy in Washington. Obukhov, who is now their number two man, went to the University of Chicago where he earned a master's degree. Yes, a number of them spoke nearly fluent English and Karpov was almost bilingual; he was certainly fluent. The military representatives, however, did not speak anything but Russian or Ukrainian.

QUESTION: In the restructuring of leadership in Russia that we have seen in the last few years, Mr. Gorbachev and others have brought a great deal more youth and change into their thinking. How does the military fit in? Has there been any change in the flexibility of the military structure?

AMBASSADOR EARLE: I don't think the military has changed.   It's a question of their influence with the individual, and they always have had a lot of influence. Twenty years ago somebody asked Marshall Gretchko, "How do you get your budget together?" and he replied, "Well, we take the total budget, we take what we want and then the others fight over the remnants." That may not be as true with Gorbachev, but I think it retains much validity. The military is very powerful and influential; in a way the Soviet Union is a military state. I was not at Vladivostok when President Ford met with Soviet Premier Brezhnev, but I am told that Brezhnev, before they completed the Vladivostok accord which gave such impetus to our negotiations, left the room several times to telephone Moscow about certain concessions he was making. The belief was that he was primarily concerned about the military reaction to what he was doing. That's why I think that Gorbachev, as the new boy, had instructions to do what he did at Reykjavik.

QUESTION: Do you think, then, that General Secretary Gorbachev might be on borrowed time, as far as his elders are concerned and that if he is displaced, we might be in a more difficult position than we are now?

AMBASSADOR EARLE: I think if he is displaced we will be much worse off. It has been said that Gorbachev's reforms and apparent openness present two problems: One is that the reforms may not work. The second problem is that they *may* work. If the reforms don't work, then a reactionary, repressive group could assume leadership. Presumably that is a throwback. If it does work, the Soviets will become stronger, more capable, and more competent.

I would like to see the Soviets dragged kicking and screaming into the twentieth century. I advocate addressing issues other than military ones; for instance, I would like to see more trade with the Soviet Union. We compete with them militarily, the one area in which they are very strong. We are stronger in every other area and we are equal with them in the military. I would like to see them try to compete with us in trade and so forth and so on. Bring them into the twentieth century because then they might be a little easier to live with.

QUESTION: After the Reykjavik proposals came out there was quite a sharp reaction by our NATO allies, as you know. This morning's *Washington Post* suggests that the reason General Bernard Rogers is not being retained is because he expressed those views quite openly. As a negotiator, what complexities are inherent in your role, and also what should be our views *vis-a-vis* NATO?

AMBASSADOR EARLE: I was at NATO when the first SALT delegation came to NATO for the first time. It was July 1969 and the delegation genuinely consulted with the North Atlantic Council, because at that time it was a new ball game. The delegation was going to see the Soviets for the first time four months later in November and they were seeking suggestions and advice from those experienced diplomats, many of whom were former ambassadors to the Soviet Union.

Throughout SALT II, I flew up to Brussels from Geneva at least once every six weeks and met with the Council to describe where we were and what we were doing. We kept them informed, but because we were negotiating central systems—ICBM launchers, SLBM launchers, heavy bombers—they weren't greatly concerned. I think they felt gratified, but they had the attitude that if it were good enough for us, then it is good enough for them. They were concerned about a noncircumvention clause because they feared that if we did not accept the Soviet proposal, it would have prevented transfers to NATO of certain weapons systems. That was their one major concern.

With the INF negotiations and the intermediate range forces, the Allies obviously have considerably more direct interest, because these weapons are not aimed at Washington and New York, but rather they are aimed at Paris, London and Madrid. Our consultation record has continued to be very good. As I said earlier, the Europeans are sometimes difficult to deal with because they are never satisfied. It is understandable. They do not want the nuclear war fought in West Germany, but on the other hand, they *do* want nuclear weapons there to prevent the war from starting. We have brought them into the discussions throughout this period of eighteen years of negotiations; I think we have kept them very well informed.

NARRATOR: Do you want to say anything about General Rogers?

AMBASSADOR EARLE: I gathered he wanted to stay; in fact, he made it quite clear he wanted to stay. Reykjavik was, I think, a near disaster, but it was the President's near disaster. I think displacing General Rogers may be a mistake because he is a very competent gentleman. Secretary General of NATO, Lord Carrington, once said, "I wish he would stay until he is a hundred," and Carrington is one of the great men of our century. So, I'm sorry he is leaving, because he has done an excellent job.

QUESTION: You mentioned Dobrynin. In Gorbachev's bringing him back to Russia with all his wealth of experience in the United States, I would think that he'd have quite an influence on Soviet policies. Have you detected that?

AMBASSADOR EARLE: I really don't know, but he does seem to be prominent. I hope Gorbachev is using his knowledge because one of the most disconcerting things I found about the Soviets (and I'm sure they found about us) is their abysmal ignorance about our system. I hope that they are listening to Dobrynin because he did spend twenty-two or twenty-three years in Washington. I assume he has some knowledge of how our system works.

NARRATOR: Would you be willing, without any reference to your own claims to this definition, to give us a profile of what you think the American arms negotiator ought to look like? What kind of temperament, what kind of military background and knowledge of science and technology, and what kind of human qualities are most essential?

AMBASSADOR EARLE: It's hard for me not to be somewhat prejudiced. I think with few exceptions, all the chief negotiators have been lawyers, including me, and I think that is a good thing because what you are really doing is representing a client. When we drafted the treaty in Geneva, we wrote all of our own statements and treaty language. So I think clarity of expression is a very important thing, and lawyers are presumably trained to have that.

I think understanding of and familiarity with the weapons systems and defense policies is important. I had refueled in a B-52, and I had been on a submarine when it launched a missile, and I had been stuck in a Minute Man silo for forty-five minutes when I was in the Defense Department, so I had some feel for what these things were all about. The Soviet civilians did not. We clearly had an advantage of comprehension when we were discussing specific weapons systems with them.

I think that the chief negotiator should have a good personal relationship with his secretary of state, because there are moments when, for reasons of timeliness or privacy, you want to get on the phone and call the secretary of state to find out something. One big advantage I had, which my Republican predecessors have not had, was access to the secretary of state. Although there was a back channel open between the secretary of state and

Ambassador Dobrynin in Washington during the Kissinger years, Alexis Johnson and Gerard Smith were never told what was going on in that channel between Kissinger and Dobrynin. I was told everything that was going on between Vance and Dobrynin. Essentially from 1969 to 1977 the American chief negotiator labored under a distinct disadvantage in that he did not know as much as his Soviet counterpart did. Whether or not you have a close relationship with the secretary of state, you ought to at least have a close enough professional relationship with him so that he has sufficient confidence and trust in you to tell you what he has said to Dobrynin or whoever that morning. When Henry Kissinger met with Gromyko in Geneva, as he did several times, he met for two days. He did not invite Alexis Johnson to any of those meetings. He would get back on his airplane without ever seeing Alex. Instead he would send one of his aides to brief Alex privately.

To go back to the criteria, you should at least have the professional confidence of the secretary of state and the president. Patience is an invaluable asset. You also have to like people, and you must be able to treat them as people.

NARRATOR: The most notable thing this morning is that Ambassador Earle hasn't changed at all. The same clarity we associate with his SALT II expositions and defense has been evident throughout today's discussion. Thank you very much.

Continuity and Change:
NSC-68 and American Foreign Policy

W. ANDREW BANKS

NARRATOR: In a brilliant essay on NSC-68 W. Andrew Banks explores the question of "who decides" in relationship to that historic document. His extensive research on the history of NSC-68 enables him to place the decision-makers in a new and original context. He determines what was a break with the past in the NSC-68 and what represents continuity. He analyzes and criticizes the prevailing theories concerning NSC-68 and comes to some rather surprising conclusions. Although this presentation has not yet been the subject of a Miller Center Forum, it seemed so germane to the question "who decides?" that it is included. As an all important strategic doctrine, it helps illuminate national defense which is the twin focus of this little volume on arms control and defense.

MR. BANKS: Since NSC-68 was drafted and approved as national security policy in 1950, it has achieved both fame and infamy. Those who consider it famous will posit that it saved the country, or even the world, from the expansionist, militaristic Soviet empire by changing the United States from a globally ambitious but idealistic nation, into a world power whose means were better able to service a realistic foreign policy. Those who consider it infamous will argue that it was the first step in an unnecessary arms race between the two postwar superpowers. They assert that the United States greatly exaggerated the Soviet military threat, either through ignorance or intent, and they claim that national security policy was thereby distorted and preoccupied with the wrong threats. In any case, both sides agree that NSC-68 was a pivot in American foreign policy, crucial not only to the years immediately following its acceptance, but also to foreign and military policy at the present.

To a degree, both sides are correct when they identify NSC-68 as the beginning of rearmament and a search for absolute security. The period in which NSC-68 was developed did just that. However, they are incorrect if they conceive the document as a radical change in policy conception or even as a change in approved policy. The document was a very dramatic, very ideological reiteration of previously articulated but largely unimplemented foreign policy formulations.

The impetus for the document was a series of international and national events during the latter months of 1949 and the first part of 1950. The Soviet Union had consolidated the Eastern zone of Germany into a satellite state, the German Democratic Republic. China had been "lost" when communist forces completed a successful revolution against an inept but American-supported nationalist government. Domestically, there was a turnover in Truman administration personnel, and persons with views more conducive to the implementation of such a policy were in positions to make national action consistent with national objectives. But the major, overriding event was the Soviet explosion of an atomic device in 1949.

The successful Soviet test sent shock-waves through the Truman administration. Soviet analysts and foreign policy experts were surprised but not because the Soviet Union had the capability to develop a nuclear weapon. What stunned them was the speed with which the technology had been diffused. The United States had not expected the Soviet Union to develop atomic capabilities until late 1951 or early 1952 at the earliest. The American nuclear monopoly was gone, and U.S. policy-makers immediately began to question whether the United States could protect itself and guard its interests in a world where it no longer held the only trump card.

On September 23, President Truman announced to the nation news of the Soviet test, and discussion began immediately as to whether the U.S. should develop the hydrogen, or "super," bomb. Accordingly, the Atomic Energy Commission (AEC) was assigned to evaluate the situation and supply a recommendation. The AEC's General Advisory Commission, with Robert Oppenheimer as chairman, submitted its recommendation to the AEC in late October, and the recommendation was that the "super" should not be developed. The advisory commission had serious reservations concerning the morality of nuclear weapons in general, and it was especially wary of approving a device many times more destructive than anything yet deployed.[1] Voting on November 9, the AEC acted to accept this recommendation.

Reaction in the Defense Department was swift. Officials there considered it a vital necessity that the United States make use of every possible technological advantage. The Joint Committee on Atomic Energy echoed these views. Attempting to reconcile the conflicting sentiments within his administration, the President designated a three-man committee of Secretary of State Dean Acheson, Secretary of Defense Louis Johnson, and AEC Chairman David Lilienthal to determine "whether and in what manner"[2] the U.S. should develop the hydrogen bomb. The committee was split among Johnson, who supported the program, Lilienthal, who did not, and Acheson, who was undecided but who agreed to follow Paul Nitze's advice to separate the decisions of development and production.[3] In January, the committee compromised on a recommendation that the feasibility of developing the bomb be studied in conjunction with an overall reappraisal of U.S. foreign policy. They submitted their report to the President on January 31. Truman accepted it and took two actions. First, he decided to continue work to determine the feasibility of thermonuclear weapons, and he announced this to the public. Second, he directed the secretaries of state and defense to

> undertake a reexamination of our objectives in peace and war and of the effect of these objectives on our strategic plans, in light of the probable fission bomb capability and possible thermonuclear bomb capability of the Soviet Union.[4]

The Secretaries subsequently established the State-Defense Policy Review Group to undertake the analysis.

Had this order not been given, the U.S. would not have been without a strategic reassessment. On January 5, 1950, the National Security Council had decided to do its own general strategic appraisal on the basis of current commitments and the strategic situation. By January 18 the State Department had set up a group to cooperate with the study. The effect of the order was to take an already initiated assessment out of NSC control.[5]

The Policy Review Group was headed by Paul H. Nitze, the director of the State Department's Policy Planning Staff (PPS), who had assumed that position upon the departure of George Kennan on January 1. The State Department was further represented by Carlton Savage, George Butler, and Harry Schwartz, all of the PPS, and Gordon Arneson, special assistant to Undersecretary James Webb, for atomic energy policy. The Defense Department was represented by Major General James H. Burns [ret.], assistant secretary of defense for foreign military affairs and liaison to the State Department; Major General T. H. Landon, Air Force Member of the Joint Strategic Survey Committee of the Joint Chiefs of Staff; Najeeb Halaby, director of the Office of Foreign Military Affairs; and Robert LeBaron, chairman of the Military Liaison Committee to the United States Atomic Energy Commission. The National Security Council was represented by James Lay, its executive secretary.

An important aspect of the Defense Department's representation was the allocation of decision-making responsibility. General Burns ruled himself and Mr. Halaby out as main spokesmen for Defense because of that department's commitment to budgetary savings and because Secretary Johnson was wary of State-Defense contact. The onus thus fell to Landon, the JSSC member. The JSSC was not, in fact, responsible to the Joint Chiefs but was merely an advisory board which submitted its views on the implications of strategic plans. So the default to Landon made possible the bypassing of inquiries by military and defense professionals. Landon came to the initial meetings supportive of existing budgets, programs, and plans, but his commitment was not firm. When the first meetings illustrated a tremendous difference between State Department and Defense Department assumptions on national and Soviet strengths and weaknesses, Landon viewed it as an invitation to break from the budget restrictions. Because he had decision-making power, the committee became united in its view that their assessment should not be made within the confines of currently available means.[6]

An interesting irony of the State Department's unconstrained economic policy was the way much of that feeling was acquired. The State Department and Defense Department had worked closely together on projects such as the European Recovery Program and the Mutual Defense Assistance Program. These interdepartmental contacts had impressed upon the State Department personnel the importance of military considerations in their foreign policy analysis. They emerged from the meetings believing that military power could be effectively synthesized with foreign policy conception.[7]

A draft was quickly readied and submitted to six special consultants for their comments. Among the more prominent were: Robert Oppenheimer; James Conant, president of Harvard University and a member of the AEC General Advisory Committee; and Robert Lovett, former Undersecretary of State. Oppenheimer, interviewed first, had four objections to the development of the hydrogen bomb. First, he believed it simply would not work. Second, he believed the research would consume too much fissionable material. Third, he believed fusion would create too great a force to convert to a practical weapon. Finally, he argued that it would demonstrate to the Soviets the feasibility of the weapon. Some years later, Nitze refuted this argument by asserting that the Soviets had produced a thermonuclear weapon before the United States.[8] Lovett thought the document did not go far enough and advocated using every means at our disposal to fight the cold war and any hot war which might develop.[9] Of the other consultants, only Conant raised serious objections, believing the goal of bringing about a fundamental change in the conduct of Soviet foreign policy was too broad. He suggested the document state the goal of attempting "to live on tolerable terms" with the U.S.S.R. for a period of twenty years.[10] Conant's objections were reversed some months later when he agreed to chair the Committee on Present Danger.[11]

Taking these comments into account, the study group scheduled a March 22 meeting with Acheson and Johnson to discuss the committee's progress and anticipated conclusions. When Secretary Johnson arrived at the meeting and Nitze began discussing the progress of the group, Johnson flew into a rage. He questioned where the authority for such a wide-ranged report had come from, and he wondered why he had not been consulted on it. He criticized the procedure for calling the discussion meeting as being outside of proper channels. He also charged that he had not been given time to read the document, and he resented being called to approve something over which he had no control. He then stormed out of the room, leaving most of those present stunned and leaving Burns in tears of humiliation.

Acheson followed Johnson into the next room, where they discussed the situation, and Acheson was able to reassure Johnson that he was not being railroaded into policy. But he also placed a call to President Truman and informed him of likely Defense Department intransigence on the project. Truman authorized Acheson to have the group proceed on its present course, thereby reaffirming the State Department's control over the entire process.

In addition to these special consultants, drafts of the report were sent to a wide array of foreign policy specialists, including Kennan, Charles Bohlen, Dean Rusk, Llewellyn Thompson, and Philip Jessup. Most of these individuals responded to the solicitation within a few days.

Thompson criticized the document because "the conclusions do not appear to follow logically from this analysis and some of the most important suggestions in the paper are not directly supported by the analysis."[12] He cited the call for increased military capability as a conclusion which was not supported by discussions of present programs. However, he did not reject the document in its entirety and agreed with most of the analyses.

A response submitted by Acting Assistant Secretary Raymond Hare questioned the "dispassionately analytical approach" taken by the draft and admonished the committee to make the "cold war into a warm war by infusing into it ideological principles to give it meaning."[13] One wonders if the now-unavailable draft was very similar to the final product. It is difficult to view NSC-68 as non-ideological.

A comparable comment was submitted by Assistant Secretary of State for Public Affairs Edward W. Barrett, who believed the proposed buildup would not be supported by present public opinion. He suggested that the atmosphere for an effective program should be created. He thought the government "should have at least the broad proposals for action in hand before the psychological 'scare campaign' is started."[14]

Two critics of the entire effort were Bohlen and Kennan, who agreed that the nature of the Soviet threat was too complex to serve as a starting point for planning military strategy or foreign policy. Although neither doubted that the Soviets, given a significant chance, would directly challenge U.S. security, they each had reservations concerning the document's emphasis on all-out war. Kennan tried but failed to make his position clear. In his attempt to explain why he considered the recommended build-up to be the wrong one, Kennan could not show the PPS how his conception of containment and policy toward the Soviets differed from theirs.[15] The difference may have been that Kennan thought a comprehensive foreign policy was too complex to be put in writing. He had "no confidence in the ability of men to define hypothetically in any useful way, by means of general and legal phraseology, future situations . . ."[16]

There were other criticisms. The goals the document stated were thought by some to be too lofty. There was concern that the economic potential of the United States as a tool in the cold war had been underestimated. Others questioned the lack of concrete information and the vague tone of the document. However, most of those consulted did agree with the basic assumptions and conclusions. The U.S.S.R. was an increasingly dangerous threat. To counter this threat, the United States had to increase its military readiness.

The document was completed in late March, while Secretary Johnson was in Europe at a NATO Defense Ministers' meeting. While he was absent, the manuscript was reviewed and approved unanimously by the JSSC, the Joint Chiefs of Staff as a group and as individuals, all the civilian chiefs of the service branches, and the Defense adviser on the AEC. It was submitted to Johnson on April

6 with the signatures of all the above persons. He was confronted with a *fait accompli*. Some time later, Nitze admitted that Johnson had been deliberately left out.[17]

Usually, such a policy proposal would proceed first to the National Security Council for discussion and approval before going to the president for his approval. Importantly, NSC-68 went directly to the President on April 7; it was not filtered through NSC discussion. This route reemphasized the influence the State Department had on policy development because what Truman saw was a draft by a State Department-dominated committee. Truman referred it to the NSC after he had reviewed it, but by then his impression had been formed. Passage to the NSC was for consideration as policy, but Truman also directed that a concurrent study be made on how to implement it, a signal that he viewed the report's conclusions favorably. His directions requested the NSC "give me a clear indication of the programs which are envisaged in the Report, including estimates of the probable cost of such programs. . . . I am concerned that action on existing programs should not be postponed or delayed."[18]

NSC-68 was not a revolutionary program of American foreign policy but a document carefully constructed to solicit a programmatic response to policies that had been enunciated by and approved with other statements. It presented arguments in sharp black and white contrast and built to conclusions in a way that eliminated alternative approaches to policy. The central theme of NSC-68 was that, in order to frustrate the Soviet design of continued expansion into the non-Soviet world, the free nations needed to develop successful political and economic systems. These systems in turn required an adequate military shield to develop properly, but this requirement was inadequate and had been neglected. Thus

> a substantial and rapid building up of strength in the free world is necessary to support a firm policy intended to check and *roll back* the Kremlin's drive for world domination.[19]

The document began by describing how recent history had destroyed the traditional world balance of power, causing power to gravitate to the United States and the Soviet Union. The U.S.S.R., following a philosophy "antithetical to our own," was attempting to "impose its absolute authority over the rest of the world."[20]

Following this was a sharp contrast of the fundamental designs of each nation, one which quoted the Declaration of Independence and the Constitution in establishing that the U.S. was fundamentally committed to preserving the freedom of the individual through a free society. The Soviets, in contrast, sought to consolidate absolute power in their own country, extend that influence to areas under their influence, and eventually destroy the nations of the non-Soviet world. The United States was the only obstacle to this design and was thus the primary target of the Soviet Union.

The emotional, ideological discussion continued by describing the United States as a nation built upon tolerance and diversity with a desire to see a world society based upon consent. This character presented the United States with a dilemma. On one hand, as a democratic society it had to accept even that diversity which threatened it from within. However, in order to protect this diversity, it was being forced to protect itself from external threats which imperiled it. The contrasting portrayal of the Soviet Union was of a regime intolerant of diversity because variance was a threat to their rule. They endeavored to eliminate those who did not share their unanimity, both within their nation and internationally.

A third sharp contrast existed between the means available to the two rivals. The Soviets were viewed as unrestrained by means; they were only respondent to expediencies. The U.S.S.R. utilized psychological, political and economic weapons in its expansion. But these tactics were enhanced greatly by the vast armed forces of the U.S.S.R., which were used to intimidate neighbors and support an aggressive foreign policy. Although actual military force had not been employed by the Soviets, they were seen as unhesitant to do so if it were the most efficient method. The United States, as a free society, was much more restricted in its available means. The role of the military was protection, although the integrity of our system will not be jeopardized by any means, covert or overt, violent or non-violent, which serve the purpose of frustrating the Kremlin design . . . provided they are appropriately calculated to that end.[21]

It is debatable as to what this passage advocates. It could conceivably mean that there were no restrictions when confronting the Soviets. Other parts of the text, however, indicate that any means were acceptable in defending oneself from the Soviet world design, but not all means were available in trying to achieve the objective of changing the conduct of Soviet foreign relations.

These sharp contrasts persisted through discussions of Soviet and American current capabilities, potential means, and probable intentions. In each instance, the Soviet Union was portrayed as a dynamic, militant force of ever-increasing danger. The United States was contrasted as a nation of enormous potential which was not sufficiently dedicated to preserving its society and the independence of its neighbors.

The contrasts led to the drafters' choice of four conclusions. The U.S. could elect to 1) continue on its present course of policy; 2) retreat into isolation; 3) initiate a preventive war: or 4) initiate the rapid build-up of strength which the document had emphasized throughout. Given these choices, there really was no choice. Wells termed the development of this inevitable conclusion "sophomoric."[22]

NSC-68 did bring some modifications to foreign policy, but most of these were of emphasis or were decisions on unresolved issues; they were not changes of substance. The first variation concerned the Soviet threat. It was not viewed as being of a different type than had previously been realized, but it was of different degree. The most widely accepted policy document before NSC-68, NSC 20/4, had given the Soviets little chance of political success West of the Luebeck-Trieste line.[23] NSC-68 reversed this line of thought. In holding that the Soviets preferred to expand their influence by political means and in asserting that an emphasis should be placed upon rebuilding the confidence of Western nations as a means to combat this political threat, it was established that the threat had either increased, returned, or had always been there. The contradiction in the reasoning was that, although the program of rebuilding the West had been largely successful, the threat had grown even greater.

A second alteration was the development of a position on the possible use of atomic weapons. The document recognized the ongoing debate as to whether a policy of "no first use" should be adopted. It stated that no such policy should be adopted because such a declaration would be interpreted as a sign of weakness by the Soviet Union. Although future use of nuclear weapons was declared an option, NSC-68 advocated a diminished reliance upon them as the primary deterrent of the Soviet Union. While stockpiles were to be expanded rapidly, they were to be outstripped in emphasis by conventional forces.

Surprisingly, the event which was the primary trigger of the study did not affect the content of national security policy. In spite of the very recent development of Soviet atomic technology, the perception as to the capability of the Soviets to deliver an atomic blow against the United States was no different than it had been two years previously. In November 1948, NSC 20/4 had forecast that the Soviets would develop by 1955 the capability of serious air attacks on the U.S. with chemical, biological, or atomic weapons.[24]

Another resolved controversy was the question of extensive basing of American military units abroad to obtain a presence at all possible critical points and to meet limited Soviet probes. In the months prior to the drafting of NSC-68, the Joint Chiefs of Staff had advocated increasing the scope of world-wide bases available to American armed forces. The PPS argued against this. Unexpectedly, the Joint State-Defense Committee, dominated by the PPS, recommended expanded basing.

A final predominantly military consideration of NSC-68 was the designation of a critical date for preparedness. NSC 20/4 had given 1955 as a time when the Soviets would have the capability to attack the United States, but this estimation was not made in light of the factor of American deterrent. It was an assessment of raw capability. NSC-68 assessed both the Soviet program of expansion of military capability and deterrent effect of U.S. forces. It reached the conclusion that if present trends were to continue, the expected Soviet attainment of 200 bombs in mid-1954 would mark a critical date for the United States.[25]

Economic assumptions concerning military budgeting were also changed during the course of NSC-68's planning. In general, the mode of thinking in which means dictated ends was broken. The document emphasized new and larger ends and sufficiency of means.[26] Critics such as Gaddis and Melanson have challenged the wisdom of such an approach, but Nitze has responded that they have misinterpreted the document.

Prior to the changes brought about by NSC-68 and the events in its aftermath, military budget planning was dictated by the limits placed on the budget as a whole and the perceived priorities of domestic programs and foreign aid. The Truman administration's method of arriving at a military budget was unrelated to military commitments or needs. Budget Director Frank Pace set a national budget ceiling, based on what the economy could stand in taxes. He then subtracted out essential domestic expenditures and foreign aid. What was left was what was available for defense.[27]

The input of the military was rejected because the president and the Congress perceived that the separate branches of the military competed as rivals within the system. Each was thought to be attempting to create a stand-alone force.[28] These perceptions were not without some basis, but they were also dangerous because they removed military planning from a rational assessment to an arbitrary determination. As a result, the military was forced to implement 1948 and 1949 programs on a basis of what others determined to be sufficiency, an estimate dependent upon misperceived economic and political feasibility.[29]

The climate for such ill-conceived planning was made possible by the widely prevailing view that the United States had only limited means of implementing foreign and military policy and that overextension of those means would lead to the internal destruction of the nation. Truman echoed this sentiment during the 1948 presidential election campaign in stating that the economy could not afford defense spending in excess of $15 billion.[30] His campaign was built on expansion of the Fair Deal, and it was assumed that the funds for this augmentation would come from military and foreign aid programs. Pace fought to reduce the ceiling even further, advocating a $13.5 billion ceiling for defense expenditures for fiscal year 1950.[31]

It was under these circumstances that the budget process began to have serious repercussions in relation to American military planning. Increasing emphasis came to be laid on the most efficient weapons—atomic ones. Military strategists warned that the proposed 1950 budget would only allow the mounting of an air attack from Great Britain in response to Soviet aggression versus Western Europe.[32] A built-in strategy of "massive retaliation" was the only deterrent available.

NSC-68 was vital because it rationalized how more funds could be devoted to the military. The fundamental assumption was that the

> capacity of the American economy to support a build-up . . . is limited not . . . so much by the ability to produce as by the decision on the proper allocation of resources to this and other resources.[33]

The method to accomplish this was expansion of the entire economy, and the report forecast that a gross national product of $300 billion, as compared to a 1949 estimate of $256 billion, could soon be reached. If such an expansion were successful, "the necessary build-up could be accomplished without a decrease in the standard of living."[34] The capabilities of the nation to expand were illustrated by the avowal that although the United States was devoting only 22 percent of its GNP to military expenditures, foreign aid, and investment, it could increase its spending to 50 percent of GNP in a crisis.[35] The United States would not only expand its available means, it would use a larger percentage of those which were available. In spite of these astounding estimates on how much the United States could devote to its military in peacetime, Nitze argues that it is "demonstrably incorrect"[36] that NSC-68 put no limit on recommended policies and paid no attention to limits of means.

The increases proposed by different officials varied widely. The PPS advised Acheson that an additional $35 billion per year should be devoted to the military. Defense planners' estimates were much less ambitious. They believed extra programs would amount to an extra $4 billion per year.[37] Such estimates were made, however, before the outbreak of the Korean War, and they reflected a plan to develop two sets of figures, one for the regular budget and one for NSC-68.[38] The Korean War changed this plan. Military operations in Korea, normal armed forces functions, and the build-up of forces were treated integrally.

In addition to changes of policy approach and resource allocation, the rhetoric of politics also changed. The discussions held during the document's planning, NSC-68 itself, and the public relations campaign initiated by the administration in the spring of 1950 all illustrated that public relations was considered to be vital. The public had grown used to defense budgets of $15 billion. If the administration planned to spend 300 percent more, or even 30 percent more, it was thought the public would need an explanation.

The language of policy texts prior to NSC-68 was vastly different from what appeared in 1950. There were no discussions of fundamental purposes, no references to antithetical regimes, and no repetitive contrast of the American system of freedom with the Soviet system of intolerance. The policy statements were dispassionate and analytical, not apocalyptic. Public language of administration officials was also subdued. One study of the rhetoric of the Truman administration noted that public discourse had been "confident and predictive" in tone reflecting confidence in prospects for success.[39] Review of the publicly released policy speeches from the first two months of 1950 shows there were no urgent calls for action, no mention of dire threat, and no discussion of the strengths of the Soviet Union versus the weakness of the West. There were instead customary references to strength as a preventive measure and aid programs to war-torn and underdeveloped countries.[40]

NSC-68's planners and the project consultants were agreed that the public would have to be educated to the new direction of foreign policy and the new emphases of the administration. Some recommended that the President issue a declaration of emergency. Others thought influential groups of men should review and certify the new "tough" policy. Still others, in the words of Assistant Secretary Barrett, called for a "scare campaign."

The document itself reflected many of these suggestions and was as much an impassioned plea to save good from evil as an analysis of national security programs. Secretary of State Acheson believed that the forcefulness of the language was not only useful but necessary. In certain circumstances, he believed "qualification must give way to simplicity of statement, nicety and nuance to bluntness, almost brutality, in carrying home a point."[41]

Apparently, Acheson considered that a non-inflammatory policy paper would not make a difference. It might be accepted, but like other policies, its implementation was unlikely. A famous quotation of the Secretary illustrates this well:

> The purpose of NSC-68 was to so bludgeon the mass mind of 'top government' that not only could the President make a decision but that the decision could be carried out.[42]

Further justification for the intensity of the language were the adjustments and sacrifices which would be asked of the American public. The electorate had put a man in the White House who had campaigned on a platform of expanding social programs. Not only would the public be asked to accept less expansion in these areas, but they would be asked to support new and expensive military programs and pay the higher taxes to finance them. In addition, the American taxpayer would be the financier of economic recovery and military aid programs throughout the world.

Several authors have targeted the language of NSC-68 for criticism. Wells calls the document "the tocsin just before the fire" and refers to it as an "amazingly incomplete and amateurish study."[43] Gaddis deems that the apparent overstatement was intentional. The arguments that were simplistic in their rationale and vague in their explanation were the only means of assuring that the goal would be accomplished. Any controversial argument or detailed discussion of necessary forces or required spending levels would have made acceptance of the document more difficult and made passage of the program associated with it much more problematic.[44]

In spite of these extremes, it was recognized that NSC-68 was intended for government officials, not the general public. Indeed, it may have been targeted for only one person, Harry Truman. The limited distribution of the document and the wide acceptance of it by those who had been exposed meant there simply were not many persons left to convince. Harry Truman, however, needed to be convinced that increased spending was not only necessary but possible.

The frequency and intensity of public statements on national security and foreign policy available in the 1950 editions of the State Department Bulletin show a change began occurring in late February. There began a noticeable, but not substantial, change in the tone and frequency of the statements.

Secretary of State Acheson was especially active, constantly emphasizing two themes. The first was American development of "situations of strength" which would bring the Soviet Union to realize that their present method of conducting foreign affairs would be unacceptable in the future. Only by changing their conduct could agreement between the U.S. and U.S.S.R. be reached. A second theme was "total diplomacy," which stressed that domestic and foreign policy were interlocked and that there was no difference between the two. The Secretary's plan was

> to continue making speeches on the subject, driving home each time the same basic points, and adding little by little to the proposals for meeting these problems.[45]

Acheson spoke before group after group, emphasizing it was "doubly acute, doubly urgent"[46] to make the system work effectively. "The system" mentioned here was considered to be one in which individual nations carried a large share of their own burdens and also one in which nations agreed to live in a community of consent. However, the system was jeopardized because the U.S.S.R. did not abide by its rules. Attempts to enforce the rules through international agreements or organizations could not curb Soviet tendencies because "Soviet behavior cannot be legislated."[47] What had to be done was convince the Soviet Union that it must accommodate itself to the world order.

After Truman reviewed the draft in April and indicated some measure of support, the rhetoric took a substantial jump in intensity. Public speeches indicated not only the importance of being strong, but the presence of a very real threat to American security and American society. The administration's "official" level of discourse was established by Acheson in an address before the American Society of Newspaper Editors. The address was announced beforehand as a major policy speech and broadcast nationally.[48] Acheson informed his audience that the U.S. was faced with a challenge to the basis of its civilization and the safety of the free world. The Soviets were identified as willing to eliminate their enemies one by one, but the United States was their principal and ultimate target. He stressed the need to broaden the consensus of policy and involve each societal member in the total diplomacy. All functions of government had to be directed toward the end of national survival.[49]

Acheson outlined six lines of action to his listeners: 1) The doctrine of freedom must be an unqualified belief of all citizens and all in government. 2) This doctrine must be widely communicated, not only among ourselves but throughout the world. 3) The country must rebuild its defenses. 4) The world economy must be rebuilt and standards of living everywhere must be raised. 5) International organizations must improve their ability to function as arenas of political cooperation and integration. 6) There would be no negotiations on a general post-war settlement until aggression was done away with.

But as much as these speeches seemed to stress the reality of a menace, they were also a warning against isolationism. John Foster Dulles accused those who supported U.S. isolationism of being the "de facto accomplices of Soviet Communism" and stressed that the creation of political unity would require "some self-restraint in exercising political freedoms and indulging in political controversy."[50] What is ironic about speeches such as these was the readiness to abandon the very principles of diversity and tolerance which NSC-68 had emphasized as being essential to the survival of our society.

The most specific statements were issued in late May, when the first public disclosures were made on the extent of Soviet military preparations, including figures on the amount of Soviet defense spending. Americans were asked to make sacrifices and the society as a whole was chastised for being lackadaisical. The call was for mobilization.[51]

In spite of this great effort to educate the public and sway opinion, several very good opportunities were missed to deliver the message. Truman himself went on a May "whistle stop" tour, which included over fifty short addresses during twelve days. This would have been a golden opportunity to push the program and garner publicity, but Truman stressed foreign policy in only two or three of the speeches.[52] Likewise, on May 5, Truman announced to the press there was no alarming possibility of a shooting war with the Soviet Union and, in fact, the world was more settled than it had been in 1946. Consequently, he announced his plan to reduce the military budget in Fiscal Year 1951.[53]

The mixed messages being sent by the administration were evident when one compared these statements on the budget and the world situation with other pronouncements. While on his multi-stop tour, Truman proclaimed that the struggle for peace in the Cold War was as important as was winning World War II because the Soviets, like the Nazis, meant to wipe out democracy.

Acheson missed an opportunity, as well. In his executive session testimony before the Senate Foreign Relations Committee, he spoke only briefly of the Soviet threat. He did confirm that a rapid buildup of forces to counter the Soviet presence in Europe needed to be completed within three or four years, but he expressed his wish to leave much of the initiative for the program to the Europeans. Most of his testimony concerned policy toward specific areas of security concern to the U.S., and rarely was there a mention of imminent threat to these areas.[54]

After the outbreak of the Korean War, rhetoric remained at a fevered pitch. It reached a high point on

December 16, when Truman declared a national state of emergency, telling the public "the increasing menace of the forces of communist aggression requires that the national defense of the United States be strengthened as speedily as possible."[55] The tone of the message was such that it gave the impression the nation was on the edge of disaster. Two days later, Truman requested that Congress grant him emergency powers of "mobilization" similar to those in Titles I and II of the first War Powers Act of 1940, which had been concerned with emergency reorganization and contracting authority, respectively.[56]

Now, all important opportunities were used to convey the message of crisis. In the ceremony celebrating the lighting of the national Christmas tree on December 24, the theme of the battle against Communism was raised.[57] A few weeks later, Truman's entire State of the Union Message was devoted to foreign policy and the Cold War. The concern was not how to ease it but how to win it. He declared, "We are preparing for full wartime mobilization, if that should be necessary."[58]

The propaganda campaign worked. By August, over half the electorate believed the United States was already involved in World War III.[59] Groups of influential persons met to discuss the world situation and what they saw as the deteriorating American position. On September 28, in what was billed as the Citizen's Conference, General Eisenhower and other university presidents met with prominent industrialists, bankers, and newsmen. The general spoke to them of the challenge ahead and what should be done to meet it. A less temporary group was the Committee on Present Danger, which lobbied the public and public officials over the fact that the United States did not possess the means of stopping the Soviet Union in Western Europe.

The final factor which distinguished NSC-68 from other policies was its implementation. The implementation of the program was not different in style or in organization. It was different simply *because it happened.* Throughout 1948 and 1949, the Policy Planning Staff and the National Security Council had prepared documents advocating an immediate and substantial buildup of American and allied strength, and most of these recommendations were approved. Invariably, domestic considerations of the budget ceiling and programs of higher priority precluded implementation. NSC-68 was different. President Truman, upon first reviewing the document, asked for the development of a program which included the measures recommended by NSC-68. Work began almost immediately.

The work of program development fell to an ad hoc committee chaired by James Lay. The committee concerned itself with three questions: the timing of the start of the proposed buildup, the broad implications of the conclusions of NSC-68, and the formulation of programs under NSC-68. As far as the first question was concerned, August 1, 1950, became the target date for a program. Before that time, agencies would be able to approach the Congress for supplemental appropriations. The question of implications was much broader, and it was determined that further interagency discussion and cooperation were needed before broad statements could be made. The third question was easily resolvable in terms of tools. Much less definite was its resolution in terms of scope.

There are several documents which demonstrate the progress made by the ad hoc committee and other actors, and most of these formulations came after the start of the Korean War. NSC 73/4, dated August 25, provided a thorough breakdown of appropriate U.S. action in the event of direct or indirect Soviet aggression in any one of several geographic areas, thus giving the United States a clearer idea of its commitments throughout the globe. NSC-68 was itself adopted as a statement of policy on September 30, 1950. It was passed as a programmatic guide for the succeeding four to five years.

The development of the program continued through the later months of 1950, and culminated with a report to the National Security Council by the executive secretary—NSC 68/3, which outlined programs and costs for the fiscal years 1951 through 1955. The agenda called for increasing the June 1952 strength target of the armed forces to 3.2 million men, up from its level of 1.5 million on June 25, 1950. The estimated peak of budget expenditures for national security programs was $70 billion for fiscal year 1952, 25 percent of GNP. To meet these goals, it was predicted that automobile production would have to be cut by 60 percent from 1950 production, and housing would need to be reduced by a third. The work force would be greatly expanded, and average working hours would considerably increase.[60]

NSC 68/3 was comprehensive. It included estimates and analyses of U.S. military programs, foreign military assistance and economic assistance, civil defense, stockpiling, and public information. It detailed these programs with the same zeal with which NSC-68 had argued their development. On December 14, 1950, the National Security Council considered the draft report NSC 68/3 and adopted the draft.

In his state of the Union Message Truman announced his requests for an active military force of three and a half million men and an increase in production capacity to 50,000 planes and 35,000 tanks per year.[61] His fiscal year 1952 budget message, delivered a few weeks later, outlined the new priorities of his administration and itemized the extent of his new program.

On June 25, 1950, the Republic of Korea (South Korea) was attacked by armed forces of the Peoples Democratic Republic of Korea (North Korea). In response to this action, Truman issued a statement that he had "ordered the U.S. air and sea forces to give the Korean government troops cover and support." He was now convinced that "Communism has passed beyond the use of subversion . . . and will now use armed invasion and war."[62] Whether termed a "police action" or a "conflict," the United States was at war.

On July 19, 1950, Truman requested that Congress approve a $10 billion supplemental defense appropriation for fiscal year 1951, which had started the first of that month. The Korean War had provided the political impetus for this request, but these funds were not only for purposes of taking part in that conflict. One estimate was that $6 billion of this amount was intended for general expansion unconnected to Korea, but other testimony indicated this estimate was high.[63] Two more supplemental requests followed. On August 4, Truman requested $1.6 billion, and on December 1, he asked for $16.8 billion, of which $9 billion was for procurement of strategic bombing hardware, equipment which was not a factor in the Korean conflict.[64]

An important note is the procedure which determined the amount of these requests. They, like previous budget estimates, were made independent of an assessment of the military force levels which were required to meet American commitments. Although one of the intents of NSC-68 had been to assert the importance of desirability over capacity by adjusting means and ends through economic mobilization, the war produced a reversal in emphases.[65]

The Korean War was the catalyst for expansion of the military program and increases in defense budgets, in spite of any impact which NSC-68 might have had. Acheson admits

> it is doubtful whether anything like what happened in the next few years could have been done had not the Russians been stupid enough to have instigated the attack against South Korea and opened the 'hate America' campaign.[66]

There are scholars who agree with Acheson. Wells estimates that had not the Korean War been initiated, the programs implemented as a result of NSC-68 would only have amounted to $3 billion annually. The perceived influence of the Soviet Union in the initiation of the war provoked the development of numerous reassessments of the Soviet threat to other parts of the world and the proper American response to any further aggression.

The most important reevaluation was NSC 73/4, a report which concluded that, although there was no reason to suspect the Soviet Union was prepared to launch a global war, the situation in Korea may have made such a scenario more likely. The paper also concluded that no evidence existed to show the U.S.S.R. would or would not initiate attacks short of global war against nations such as Finland, the Middle East, or the Balkans. Russian troops might also appear in Korea, as they had not yet been introduced there. The Soviet use of proxy forces was raised as a possibility in regard to West Germany, Austria, Yugoslavia, Greece, and Turkey.

The proposed response by the United States to limited Soviet attacks was to be action "with varying degrees of risk."[67] In Iran, Greece, or Turkey, the United States would deploy "such forces as can be made available without jeopardizing the United States security."[68] On the other hand, if Soviet action were taken in Finland or Afghanistan, the United States would take no military action. Likewise, Chinese action in the Far East was not to be met by an American military response. Any situation which might require a military response was further limited by the requirement that the Department of Defense be consulted beforehand "as to the military soundness of the decision in light of the military commitments and capabilities existent at the time."[69] The implications of such a policy on standard interpretations of NSC-68 are to deny that NSC-68 and its related analyses intended for universalization of U.S. security interests.

The Korean War was the factor of greatest influence in bringing about the changes in foreign policy and in catalyzing implementation. There were other factors, however, which played a subsidiary role. Previous international events had contributed to create a climate of apprehension about Soviet intentions. They included Russian development of an atomic bomb, the installation of a Chinese communist regime, the Treaty of Friendship and Cooperation signed between the Soviet Union and the People's Republic of China, the Berlin blockade, the Czechoslovakian coup, and the creation of the German Democratic Republic.

In the domestic realm, the anti-communist campaign of Senator Joe McCarthy had begun in February of 1950. McCarthy's hysterical charges and random persecutions set the stage for any policy that was strongly anti-Soviet because whoever opposed taking strong action against Soviet communism was himself open to charges of being a sympathizer. Specific charges were made against the State Department, and one might assume that these charges were an influence on the tone of Acheson's rhetoric in the spring of 1950.

The first important change in personnel occurred when Secretary of State George Marshall left the Department and was replaced by Dean Acheson. Marshall had been committed to the concept of limited military spending and never supported former Defense Secretary James Forrestal in his bid to break the long-range budget ceiling of $15 billion imposed in 1948. As the person with whose name the postwar reconstruction of Europe had most closely been associated, Marshall was devoted to economic rehabilitation rather than military armament.

Acheson brought different views to the job. He did not believe that economic recovery and stability would be enough. Without military power, he thought strong economies would be swept away. This was typical of Acheson's conception of international relations, which he judged were predominantly conditioned by considerations of power. In Gaddis Smith's examination of Acheson, the author concludes that military power had immediate or ultimate bearing on all his work as secretary of state. Each decision was tested by that gauge.[70]

Acheson's difference with Marshall on the issue of how military spending affected the economic health of the nation may be illustrated by his instructions to PPS Directors Kennan and Nitze. He instructed both to provide continuous advice on the possible actions which would best serve U.S. security interests and to provide this advice without regard to domestic acceptability.[71] In other words, he was an advocate of determining ends first and acquiring the means to accomplish them. And the ends he envisioned were quite expansive. He wanted the United States to assume what had traditionally been the British place in the world—that of peacemaker, organizer, and civilizer.[72]

Acheson strongly maintained that the ability of the West to discourage Soviet attack could not be reliant solely upon an atomic deterrent because nuclear weapons, even if used on Russian territory, would not stop a Soviet advance. With or without nuclear weapons, conventional forces would be required.[73] At the same time, the importance of atomic weapons to the overall deterrence network advocated by Acheson was reflected in his position that stockpiling of such weapons was not just important, but essential.

A second major personnel change was Louis Johnson's replacement of James Forrestal as Defense secretary in March of 1949 and Johnson's subsequent departure late in 1950. Before he left, Forrestal had become concerned with the declining capabilities of the United States in light of the perceived Soviet potential, and he was therefore an advocate of lifting the $15 billion ceiling.[74] Johnson, however, was committed to keeping the defense establishment and the defense budget down. He declared,

"We have not maintained and will never maintain at all times armed forces large enough to win a major war. Such a policy would be economically suicidal and inconsistent with our democratic process."[75]

The irony of Johnson's policies on budgeting and contact between the State and Defense Departments was the way they resulted in policies he did not want. His refusal to allow intimate State-Defense contacts and his hostility towards increased spending pushed the decision-making apparatus away from him and toward the State Department.

A third change was the replacement of Edwin Nourse as chairman of the Council of Economic Advisers with Leon Keyserling. Nourse was another policy-maker who believed there was a limit to the amount the United States could spend on its military and still maintain a strong society. Keyserling's conception was radically different. He thought that instead of adjusting the way the economic pie was divided among priorities, the size of the economic pie could be adjusted to achieve all goals.[76]

Another member of the Truman administration who played an important role in influencing the implementation of NSC-68 was Robert Murphy, who replaced Clark Clifford at the White House as Special Counsel to the President. Following Clifford's departure in the fall of 1949, the White House staff lacked presidential advisers with broad policy-making experience. Consequently, these advisers looked to others for advice, and Murphy in particular accepted the arguments of Budget Directors James Webb and Frank Pace that the capabilities of the United States were limited by her economy. Upon being briefed by the joint State-Defense Committee on the nature and extent of the threat the nation faced, he grew alarmed and came to doubt the validity of the budget ceiling.[77]

The last important personnel change was Paul Nitze for George Kennan as head of the PPS. Allegedly, Kennan left because he had grown dissatisfied with the growing militarism of American diplomacy.[78] Nitze differed greatly from Kennan in his conception of how the Soviet threat would present itself and how it should be met. The best illustration of the difference can be seen in their respective reactions to a Defense Department briefing on U.S. military preparedness. In that briefing, they were informed that

U.S. forces did not have the means to support effective military deterrents to small, local aggressions and also support forces necessary to repel a full-scale attack. A choice had to be made, and military planners chose to rely on defense against global attack.

This ran counter to Kennan's conception of how best to contain the Soviet Union. He believed the United States should develop small, unified forces that were well trained, mechanized, and highly mobile. This could be done within the $13.5 billion budget by concentrating more on the Army and allocating fewer resources to the Navy and Air Force. These small units would be able to deter Soviet aggression on the level Kennan considered them likely.

Nitze was distraught not only by the lack of preparation for limited encounters, but he was also disturbed that American preparation for large wars, even though it was the only preparation, was insufficient. Like Acheson, he believed that military force was the prime factor of influence in international relations. In his mind, the presence of nuclear weapons had not altered the fundamental nature of war.[79] War would not be limited simply by the fact that one or both sides possessed nuclear arms. Therefore, it was unwise to depend on the fact that small engagements would be the only ones faced.

The difference between the ideas of George Kennan and Paul Nitze, the way these differences affected American foreign policy during the Truman administration, and the manner in which the conceptions have continued alternately to be utilized by presidents has been the subject of lengthy study by John Gaddis. It is Gaddis' contention that Paul Nitze, unlike George Kennan, never developed the necessary strategic conception for policy that properly identified interests before it identified threats and determined means before it determined ends.

Kennan's strategy was the three-pronged method of containment: to prevent vital areas from falling under Soviet influence, to try to reverse Soviet influence in areas presently under their control, and to attempt to change some Soviet conceptions on foreign policy in general. The strategy hinged on protecting the areas of large military-industrial capability that Kennan felt could not fall into

Soviet hands: the United States, Great Britain, Germany, and Japan.

Gaddis emphasizes that Kennan's strategy was "asymmetrical." The underlying assumption of asymmetry was that the United States should determine which areas it would choose to make of vital interest, an assessment to be made independent of Soviet threats. We would then apply the means of our choosing to try to influence the situation. According to Kennan, the best available means for the United States was economic aid because this would help the nations receiving it to develop strong economies and become independent centers of power, resistant to the mainly political threat the Soviet Union presented.

Gaddis claims that NSC-68 illustrated a "failure of strategic perception"[80] in not relating its short-term goals to long-term objectives. For instance, he argues that the proposed buildup would have enhanced national security if interests had remained stable, but interests were expanded by the new formulation. Likewise, the call for attempts to fragment the Soviet empire was good, but fragmentation could not be accomplished if all Communist nations were treated the same. Third, attempting to create a moderate Soviet attitude was a commendable long-term objective, but it could not be accomplished if an anti-negotiation attitude was maintained.[81]

NSC-68 also changed the nature of the threat, according to Gaddis. No longer was it the predominantly political threat envisioned by Kennan. It was now a combined threat, a very real military threat and a political threat that was made possible primarily by an intimidating military presence. Actual power was not the only thing which mattered. The perception of power was important also.

His largest criticism is reserved for NSC-68's encouragement of symmetry, which would have had the United States confront the Soviet Union whenever and wherever it presented a threat to any nation's security. All interests became vital; there was no difference between center and periphery. Gaddis argues that the Truman administration thus lost sight of its objective: to end the cold war. "Process triumphed over policy."[82] Melanson concurs and sees the beginnings of flexible response in

Nitze's formulations. He viewed NSC-68 as regarding every communist threat as one requiring a calibrated U.S. response—conventional, nuclear, or both.[83]

The proposed relationship between threat and policy means was criticized because it too greatly expanded the means necessary and the methods available to conduct foreign policy. It found "all means affordable, all means justifiable."[84] Again Melanson agrees, charging that Nitze believed the crisis to be "a moral problem so big that traditional geopolitical calculations were not sufficient. Our potential power liberates us from conditions."[85] Nitze takes exception to analyses such as these, rebutting that NSC-68 did not foresee that U.S. means would yield unlimited options.[86]

The debate over the differences between the strategies of Kennan and NSC-68 do not end there. Whittle Johnston, a harsh critic of Gaddis and staunch supporter of the views of NSC-68, refuses to accept that Kennan's theories were possessed of a "strategic logic" that transcended time. He argues that Gaddis' criticism of the policies encouraged by NSC-68 was unfounded because Gaddis compares policy failures under NSC-68 guidelines with the policy conceptions of Kennan, while not proving that Kennan's strategy would have produced a different result. Gaddis is also taken to task for saying that Kennan was proved right in his assertions on our loss of the atomic monopoly and the discounting of the loss of China. Kennan's strategy had nothing to do with the policy followed in the cases. Johnston argues there is nothing to show Kennan's strategy would not have failed. Johnston summarizes these two points by stating that Gaddis' "causal explanations are dual and divergent."[87]

Johnston appreciates NSC-68 because it "was a brilliant effort to integrate the multiple dimensions of America's power to one another."[88] He shows that even Gaddis realized that NSC-68 was not dependent on military means, and illustrates how it showed merely that economic and political strength were not sufficient. As for the document's wider range of geographical inclusion, Johnston argues that protection of any strongpoint would necessitate protection of the periphery around it.

What both Gaddis and Johnston fail to emphasize is the distinction between strategist and strategy. Prior to the development of NSC-68, it is assumed that the strategist, Kennan, was synonymous with the strategy, namely containment. NSC-68, therefore, is viewed as a reversal of Kennan. In fact, that is not the case at all. The conceptions of foreign policy contained in NSC-68 do not begin with that document. The basic assumptions contained in NSC-68 had been part of official foreign policy statements for almost two years prior to the initiation of the NSC-68 process, and some of these statements were drafted by the Policy Planning Staff under the direction of George Kennan. It is only through the neglect of these continuities of foreign policy that NSC-68 gains significance as a policy conception and infamy as the impetus for globalization and institutionalization of the cold war.

Documents on American foreign policy reflect many continuities between NSC-68 and preceding policy: the nature of Soviet objectives, capabilities, and methods; the general objectives of U.S. foreign policy; the limits of American capacity and the extent of U.S. commitments; the means which were emphasized; and the actions recommended to pursue goals.

The fundamental design of the Soviet regime was identified as the consolidation of power, first in the Soviet Union and then in areas under that nation's control. The achievement of this objective was thought to be dependent on extension of Soviet authority and elimination of all opposition. The drafters of NSC-68 saw the ultimate Russian design as "The complete subversion or forcible destruction of the machinery of government and structure of society in the countries of the non-Soviet world," through the imposition of its authority over the rest of the world.[89]

Some argue that previous policy did not take the dynamic needs of the Soviet system to this extreme. Bohlen, and certainly Kennan, agreed that the Soviet regime did in fact need to expand to maintain its credibility, but neither concurred with the extrapolation that the ultimate goal of Soviet policy was world domination. Bohlen had objected when this was specifically stated as the prime Soviet objective in an early draft of NSC-68. This is the first case where strategists cannot be confused with policy, because the ultimate objective of the Soviet Union had been identified as world domination in several earlier documents.

NSC-7, drafted in March 1948 and seen as worthy of approval by Kennan's PPS, specifically stated that the U.S.S.R.'s ultimate objective was world domination.[90] Likewise, NSC 20/4, drafted by the PPS, identified the ultimate Soviet objective as "domination of the world." It stated that the U.S.S.R. sought a reduction in the strength and numbers of non-communist nations.[91] Perhaps important here was use of the word "reduction" as opposed to the word "elimination," which appeared in NSC-68. There was a change in degree of domination, but there was no change in substance.

The second area of perceived change from previous policy to NSC-68, at least as concerns the U.S.S.R., was the type of threat that nation represented and the emphasis it placed on different methods. NSC-68 held that the Soviet threat was multi-dimensional, one not only of military and political characteristics, but also existing as a threat of perception. The Soviet arms buildup was not only for military purposes, but was

> seeking to create overwhelming military force, in order to back up infiltration with intimidation. . . . to demonstrate to the free world that force and the will to use it are on the side of the Kremlin, that those who lack it are decadent and doomed.

It also warned of the "great coercive power for use in time of peace in furtherance of its objectives" which served "as a deterrent to the victims of its aggression from taking any action in opposition to its tactics which would risk war."[92] NSC-68 cautioned that this might produce a state of confusion and inaction in the Western world, locking it into "a descending spiral of too little and too late, of doubt and recrimination."

The relative weight assigned to the various Soviet threats gave the political and ideological threat the greatest emphasis and downplayed the immediate military threat, although it did warn of a critical year of military danger if present policy was continued. These different tools were assessed as being ready for use solely on the basis of expediency. The Soviets were viewed as being driven by militancy, but NSC-68 acknowledged that the U.S.S.R. had thus far "followed the sound principle of seeking maximum results with minimum risks and commitments."[93]

The relationship among these threats in NSC-68 and their similarity with other policy documents can be determined by the presence within NSC-68 of the verbatim conclusions of NSC 20/4. NSC 20/4 had vaguely concluded that the "gravest threat to the security of the United States within the foreseeable future stems from the hostile designs and formidable power of the U.S.S.R. . . . ." However, greater specificity was provided by subsequent statements which listed political, economic, and psychological warfare before military aggression as threats. The judgment was that "the Soviet leaders probably do not intend deliberate armed action involving the United States at this time," although "possibility of such deliberate resort to war cannot be ruled out."[94] An observation of NSC 20/4 which was not included in NSC-68 was that a careful weighing of factors points to the probability the Soviet Union was seeking to achieve its goals primarily by political means.[95]

Throughout other policy papers, there had been consistency in the assessment of the likelihood of Soviet military attack. An April 1948 report had predicted that the Soviet Union would not resort to military action in the immediate future if it could still accomplish its objectives by other means.[96] Four months later, NSC 20/2 gave five convincing arguments why the Soviets would not attack, including a preference for political means, although it did caution that "war must be . . . regarded . . . as a possibility . . . serious enough to be taken account of fully in our military and political planning."[97]

Although these documents indicate that Soviet military aggression was not anticipated at the time, factors were identified which cautioned against overconfidence. The American Embassy in Moscow reported that although the Soviets would not attack if they felt they could reach their goals by other means, conditions could arise in one or two years which would make other Soviet methods ineffective. Likewise, NSC 20/2 identified the failure of Russian political moves and Western progress as a Soviet incentive for war.

Finally, NSC 20/4 gave the Soviets "little chance of effecting at this juncture the political conquest of any countries west of the Luebeck-Trieste line."[98]

NSC-68 devoted a great deal of effort and space to assessing the various capabilities of the Soviet Union—political, economic, military, and atomic. The prominence of these assessments disturbs Gaddis, who criticizes the authors for not grasping that capabilities are a function of intention and vice versa. He argues that NSC-68 does not acknowledge they are interrelated and do not exist without each other.[99] Nitze takes issue with Gaddis. Through the late 1970s, he was firm in his belief that NSC-68 had not been overly pessimistic about the position of the international community in light of the Soviet threat because ability and intention are separate things.[100]

NSC-68 estimated that Soviet political and psychological capabilities were formidable. Exploiting militancy, revolutionary doctrine, traditional Russian imperialism, and its unchallenged dictatorial position, the Soviet regime was attempting to increase power and influence as quickly as possible. Ideology, though scorned by the Soviet citizenry, found listeners in a developing world impressed by rapid Soviet advancement. Paradoxically, NSC-68 viewed nationalism as the source of greatest Soviet psychological vulnerability due to the coercive and demanding nature of Russian domination, but it also identified the Soviet system as "monolith" held together by an "iron curtain around it and iron bars within it."[101]

Melanson has written that NSC-68 postulated that the United States could not afford to wait on nationalism and rely on a policy of fragmentation.[102] He is correct in that the United States did not choose to rely on fragmentation. He fails to give credit to the fact that NSC-68 regarded nationalism as one of the fundamental weaknesses of the Soviet system.

Economically, NSC-68 predicted that the Soviet Union would begin to close the wide gap in economic production between itself and the United States because it devoted such a large amount of resources to investment. It was on a maximum production basis, utilizing every resource possible to increase its overall strength, particularly its war-making capacity.[103]

Militarily, the Soviet Union was judged to possess military forces well in excess of those needed for defensive purposes. It was believed that Soviet leaders did not consider these forces as yet sufficient to initiate a war involving the United States. However, the West believed the Russians so fully prepared and mobilized they could

> overrun Western Europe, with the possible exception of the Iberian and Scandinavian Peninsulas; drive toward the . . . Middle East; . . . launch air attacks against the British Isles; . . . attack selected targets with atomic weapons, . . . including . . . the United States.[104]

After completing these campaigns and consolidating its gains, the U.S.S.R. could move on other areas, including Britain, the Near and Middle East, and the Iberian and Scandinavian Peninsulas.

The atomic capabilities of the Soviet Union were deemed difficult to judge accurately, but CIA estimates assign ranges of ten to twenty bombs by mid-1950, forty-five to ninety by mid-1952, and 200 by mid-1954. Because the ability of the Soviet Union to deliver these bombs was estimated at 40-60 percent, the 1954 date held significance because it represented a Soviet ability to deliver 100 bombs against the United States.

Previous national security policy had not differed substantially in its estimates of Soviet military capabilities. NSC-7 warned that the U.S.S.R. could control Europe within months and hold it for two years, that the U.S.S.R. would give strong consideration to using any atomic weapons they possessed and that the Soviet economy could support a European occupation.

NSC 20/4 saw the Soviet Union as building its war potential in anticipation of the "inevitable" war between communist and capitalist nations. It estimated that the U.S.S.R. was capable of overrunning all of continental Europe and the Near East to Cairo within six months. It also warned the Soviets would be able to complete "serious air attacks" against the U.S., and such attacks could include atomic weapons.

Just as NSC-68 had been consistent on a wide range of very important points with regard to the Soviet conduct of foreign relations, it was also consistent with previous judgments as to the best U.S. responses. NSC-68 was not substantially different from previous policy on the general objectives of U.S. foreign policy, the meaning of containment, the areas of the world whose strength was emphasized, the degree to which the United States needed to build its military forces, and the American attitude toward negotiations.

NSC-68 identified the primary American objectives as frustrating the Soviet design and inducing the U.S.S.R. to exist in a world society based on the principle of consent. The method of accomplishing this would be the development of the moral and material strength of the free world. Such strength would convince the Soviets of the futility of their plans. The language of the document was such that these objectives became a legalistic and moralistic approach to foreign and international relations. The sharp distinctions the document drew between the "free" and "slave" states was indicative of this. It is confirmed by the documents declaration that "Our overall policy at the present time may be described as one designed to foster a world environment in which the American system can survive and flourish."[105]

If the United States were to attempt to create a *pax Americana*, it would necessarily have to reject the isolationism which had at times plagued it. NSC-68 proclaimed that the objective of creating a world system in which the American system would flourish "rejects the concept of isolation and affirms the necessity of our positive participation in the world community."[106] The danger of our present policies, as identified by NSC-68, was that it would lead to this very isolation through progressive withdrawal.

In demanding more than participation, NSC-68 also ruled out only defensive participation because "it is not an adequate objective merely to seek to check the Kremlin design."[107] The consistency of this objective is clear from the statement in NSC-68 that

The objectives outlined in NSC 20/4 and quoted in Chapter X, are fully consistent with the objectives stated in this paper, and they remain valid. The growing intensity of the conflict which has been imposed upon us, however, requires the changes of emphasis and the additions that are apparent . . . the intensifying struggle requires us to face the fact that we can expect no lasting abatement of the crisis unless and until a change occurs in the nature of the Soviet system.[108]

The rejection of a defensive posture was clear even before NSC 20/4, as NSC-7 maintained that a defensive policy would be inadequate to stop Kremlin aggression. The concept of attempting to bring about a change in the Soviet system was not innovative, either. NSC 20/1, prepared in August of 1948 by the PPS, advocated attempting to reduce the power of the Soviet Union to a level at which they were no longer a threat and attempting to bring about changes in the theory and practice of relations observed by Russia.[109]

A catch-phrase which could be applied as a link between NSC-68-advocated policy and previous policy is "situations of strength," the term used throughout the spring of 1950 by Secretary of State Acheson. NSC-68's preoccupation with strengthening the Western world to illustrate to the Soviets the poor chances for their own success is the document's elaboration of the concept of "situations of strength." In August 1948, NSC 20/1 was explicit on this point, stating that the U.S. should try to "create situations which will compel the Soviet Union to recognize the practical undesirability of acting on its present precepts."[110] These exact words were present in NSC 20/4 and NSC-68.

The reputation of NSC-68, that it relied almost exclusively on military means, is undeserved. The goals were instead to "make ourselves strong, both in the way in which we affirm our values in the conduct of our national life, and in the development of our political and economic strength" and to build "a successfully functioning political and economic system in the free world."[111] It was these themes, moral and material in strength, which were repeated so often. There was no exclusive reliance upon military means, although military strength was seen as a requisite shield behind which economic and political institutions could develop.

The counter-offensive of NSC-7 included a strengthening of the military potential of the United States through compulsory military service, reconstruction of the armaments industry, and an effort to strengthen the non-Soviet world. The tools to be used included programs such as the European Recovery Program, Western European Union, and an enhanced ideological campaign.

NSC-68 identified containment as blocking further Soviet expansion, exposing the falsities of Soviet dogma, influencing a retraction of Soviet influence, and fostering the seeds of destruction within the Soviet system. As originally developed, containment would protect only vital areas of military potential. Gaddis alleges that NSC-68 reversed policy by making all interests vital. He quotes the document as follows: "The assault on free institutions is world-wide now, and in the context of the present polarization of power a defeat of free institutions anywhere is a defeat everywhere."[112] He reinforces this impression by putting it in tandem with another:

> any further substantial extension of the area under the domination of the Kremlin would raise the possibility that no coalition adequate to confront the Kremlin with greater strength could be assembled.[113]

The two quotations are not, however, reinforcing. The operative word in the second quote is "substantial," not "any." Kremlin influence over a small nation of limited power would not risk the possibility that an "adequate" coalition could not be gathered. Such a change would only occur if the U.S.S.R. gained control over an area of military-industrial importance. This very concept is indicated by the context within which the second quotation appears in NSC-68. It is used in the context of a changed balance of power and refers to the fact that the more nearly zero-sum distribution of power will not allow major realignments while maintaining stability. This does not mean the United States would not support or aid threatened nations. It only means the U.S. would not use its own military forces in all cases.

The emphasis on maintaining control of major centers of power is emphasized by the document's concern with strengthening European and Western industrial nations. As the United States gained its confidence, purpose, and direction, these qualities were supposed to be evoked in Western Europe. The recommended foreign economic policy listed assistance to Western Europe as its first feature. It was only the potential power of Eurasia which was viewed as strategically unacceptable to the United States. Finally, as was mentioned above, American military plans developed after NSC-68 and after the Korean War began did not include a universalization of security interests worthy of American military protection.

This point had been made in NSC-7, which stated that there were in Europe and Asia areas of great power, which if added to the strength of the Soviet Union would enable it to become so superior that chances for American survival would be slight. NSC 20/4 echoed that Soviet possession of Europe and the Near East, which could be accomplished in six months, would be an "unacceptable threat."[114] There were no mentions of how losses in Southeast Asia or Africa would affect the balance of power.

Although the general strengthening of societies was identified as the most important goal of policy, NSC-68's evaluation of the necessity of rapidly building the military potential of the United States should not be discounted. NSC-68 looked no longer for sufficiency of strength but absolute strength. Its importance is illustrated by the drafters' opinion that "without *superior* aggregate military strength . . . a policy of containment . . . is no more than a policy of bluff." A similar passage reads "This government cannot afford . . . to operate on a narrow margin of strength. A democracy can compensate for its natural vulnerability only if it maintains *clearly superior* overall power in its most inclusive sense." The premise was applicable not only to conventional arms but also to atomic weapons. "Only if we had *overwhelming atomic superiority* and obtained command of the air might the U.S.S.R. be deterred from employing its atomic weapons as we progressed toward the attainment of our objectives."[115]

NSC-68's stance on the vital importance of a military force of unquestioned power was not a novel concept. The Moscow Embassy report identified the only deterrent as preponderant strength. NSC 20/2 foreshadowed even the language of NSC-68 in stating that "it is necessary that we keep ourselves in a state of unvacillating mental preparedness. Without military preparedness, this would be a sham." It advocated that a military force be maintained such that there would appear to the Soviets to be little possibility of final victory.[116] Finally, a March 30, 1949, report on Measures Required to Achieve U.S. Objectives with Respect to the U.S.S.R. proposed readiness adequate for immediate commitments and rapid mobilization, with an extension to all-out war without delay.[117]

Lastly, NSC-68 has been identified as the document that eliminated the possibility of negotiation. In fact, the document did severely limit the scope of any possible negotiations between the United States and the Soviet Union but was not the originator of this position. NSC-68 held that negotiations could only take place to register situations; they could not be used to settle situations. A general settlement was possible only if it could "record the progress which the free world will have made in creating a political and economic system in the world so successful that the frustration of the Kremlin's design for world domination will be complete."[118] Negotiation, according to NSC-68, had three roles: to show that the Soviet Union cannot participate in meaningful negotiations unless a radical change occurs in the Soviet system, to record Soviet acceptance of the new political, economic, and psychological conditions of the world, and to aid in the building up of the strength of the free world by conducting negotiations without the involvement of the U.S.S.R. but with the involvement of nations such as Germany and Austria.

The position of NSC-68 on negotiations was merely a clarification of an attitude the Truman administration had held for over a year, according to Gaddis. The position was of greater utility than simple policy guidance. The refusal to negotiate was a domestic signal that the international situation had deteriorated to the point where the programs envisioned by NSC-68 needed to be implemented. Admitting negotiation was possible would dry up support for the defense program.[119]

The innovative nature and policy impact of NSC-68 has been overestimated by many. The nature of the threat, the tools used by the threatening nation, and the proposed actions to respond to that threat were all consistent with policy from 1948. Most of the arguments and recommendations of the document had appeared in similar form in another or several other documents. Especially telling is the word for word repetition of NSC 20/4 in stating NSC-68's objectives and conclusions.

What was different about the document was its rhetoric. Instead of an analytical evaluation of policy, NSC-68 was a manifesto pitting good against evil. Its arguments did not allow any conclusion but the one reached. The emotional, repetitious, dire tone of the document did exactly what Secretary of State Dean Acheson hoped it would—it "bludgeoned" the mind of top government.

The mind of top government was the second change from previous policy. Important personnel changes put into policy-implementing positions persons committed to building the military strength of the nation and suspicious of the budget ceilings which had dominated strategic and military planning. In short, assumptions of what we should do did not change. Assumptions of what we could do did change.

Third, international and domestic events provoked within the American public a paranoia it had never experienced. It was at war, and for the first time, it had enemies that could overcome the geographical barriers that had protected it. Within, it grew suspicious, vindictive and somewhat xenophobic, and it sought to have these fears exorcised by becoming strong once again.

These three factors are the true stories of policy development in the early 1950s, not NSC-68. That study just happened to be in the right place at the right time.

ENDNOTES

1. Gaddis Smith, *Dean Acheson*, in series on *The American Secretaries of State and Their Diplomacy*, volume XVI, edited by Robert H. Ferrell, (New York: Cooper Square Publishers, Inc., 1972), p. 152.

2. Smith, p. 154.

3. Samuel F. Wells, Jr., "Sounding the Tocsin," *International Security*, (4), 2, Fall 1979, p. 118.

4. *Foreign Relations of the United States* (hereafter referred to as *FRUS*), 1950, volume I, pp. 141-142.

5. Paul Y. Hammond, "NSC-68: Prologue to Rearmament," in *Strategies, Politics, and Defense Budgets*, edited by Warner Schilling, Paul Y. Hammond, and Glen R. Snyder, (New York: Columbia University Press, 1962), p. 295.

6. Wells, pp. 296-303.

7. Fred M. Kaplan, "Our Cold War Policy, Circa '50," *New York Times Magazine*, May 18, 1980, p. 89.

8. Paul H. Nitze, "The Development of NSC-68," *International Security*, (4), 4, Spring 1980, p. 176.

9. *FRUS*, 1950, I, 196-200.

10. *FRUS*, 1950, I, p. 177.

11. Wells, p. 129.

12. Thompson to the Secretary, *FRUS*, 1950, I., p. 213.

13. Hare to Undersecretary Webb, *FRUS*, 1980, I, pp. 220-221.

14. Barrett to the Secretary, *FRUS*, I, p. 226.

15. Wells, pp. 310-314.

16. George F. Kennan, *Memoirs 1925-1950*, (Boston: Little, Brown, and Company, 1967), p. 408.

17. Kaplan, p. 91.

18. NSC-68, *FRUS*, 1950, I, p. 235.

19. *Ibid.*, p. 282.

20. *Ibid.*, p. 237.

21. *Ibid.*, p. 243-44.

22. Wells, p. 139.

23. NSC 20/4, *FRUS*, 1948, volume I, part 2, p. 664.

24. *Ibid.*, p. 665.

25. NSC-68, *FRUS*, 1950, I, p. 251.

26. Hammond, p. 320.

27. *Ibid.*, p. 328.

28. *Ibid.*, p. 268.

29. *Ibid.*, pp. 274-76.

30. Wells, p. 123.

31. Hammond, pp. 279-80.

32. *Ibid.*, p. 267.

33.   NSC-68, *FRUS*, 1950, I, p. 256.

34.   *Ibid.*, p. 258.

35.   *Ibid.*, p. 286.

36.   Nitze, "The Development of NSC-68," p. 174.

37.   Smith, p. 62.

38.   Hammond, p. 354.

39.   Alan Theoharis, "The Rhetoric of Politics," in *Politics and Policies of the Truman Administration*, edited by Barton J. Bernstein, (Chicago: Quadrangle Books, 1970), p. 233.

40.   An examination of speeches released in the *Department of State Bulletin* for the period reveals a low frequency of statements on national security and general policy and low ideological intensity of language.

41.   Dean Acheson, *Present at the Creation*, (New York: W.W. Norton and Co., Inc., 1969), p. 375.

42.   *Ibid.*, p. 374.

43.   Wells, p. 139, 138.

44.   Gaddis, p. 99.

45.   Acheson memo, March 24, 1950, *FRUS*, 1950, I, p. 209.

46.   Acheson before the Senate Foreign Relations Committee, *Department of State Bulletin* (hereafter referred to as *DSB*), volume 22, number 558, March 13, 1950, p. 403.

47.   Acheson Press Conference, *DSB*, (22), 555, February 20, 1950.

48. *The New York Times*, April 23, 1950.

49. Acheson to the American Society of Newspaper Editors, *DSB*, (22), 565, May 1, 1950, p. 674-677.

50. Dulles to American Society of International Law, *DSB*, (22), 566, May 8, 1950, pp. 717-720.

51. The best example is John Foster Dulles' speech to the International House on May 16. *DSB* (22), 569, May 29, 1950, pp. 862-63 and 873.

52. Public Papers of Harry S Truman (hereafter referred to as *TPP*), 1950, pp. 296-415.

53. *New York Times*, May 5, 1950.

54. *Reviews of the World Situation, 1949-1950*, Senate Committee on Foreign Relations, Executive Session Testimony, 81st Congress, Washington: 1974.

55. *TPP*, 1950, p. 746.

56. *Ibid.*, 1950, p. 749.

57. *Ibid.*, 1950, p. 759.

58. *Ibid.*, 1950.

59. Wells, p. 141.

60. NSC 68/3, *FRUS*, 1950, I., pp. 427-429.

61. *TPP*, 1051, pp. 6-14.

62. *TPP*, 1950, p. 492.

63. Hammond, p. 253.

64. *Ibid.*, p. 356.

65. *Ibid.*, p. 354-55.

66.   Acheson, p. 374.

67.   NSC 73/4, *FRUS*, 1950, volume I, p. 384.

68.   *Ibid.*, p. 387.

69.   *Ibid.*, p. 389.

70.   Smith, p. 138.

71.   Paul H. Nitze, "The Role of the Learned Man in Government," *The Review of Politics*, (20), 3, July 1958, p. 279.

72.   Smith, p. 144.

73.   Nitze, p. 172.

74.   Hammond, p. 276.

75.   Kaplan, p. 89.

76.   John Lewis Gaddis, *Strategies of Containment*, (New York: Oxford University Press, 1982), p. 94.

77.   Hammond, p. 328.

78.   Alan Tonelson, "Nitze's World," *Foreign Policy*, (35), Summer 1979, p. 75.

79.   *Ibid.*, p. 80, 82.

80.   Gaddis, p. 106.

81.   *Ibid.*, p. 106.

82.   *Ibid.*, p. 88.

83.   Richard H. Melanson, "Paul H. Nitze to Norman Podheretz: The Tradition of Anti-Communist Containment," in *Traditions, and Values: American Diplomacy 1945 to Present*, edited by Kenneth W.

Thompson, (Lanham, MD: University of America Press, 1984), p. 154.

84. Gaddis, p. 95.

85. Melanson, p. 154.

86. Nitze, "The Development of NSC-68," p. 175.

87. Whittle Johnston, "The Containment of John Gaddis," *The National Interest*, Winter 1986/7, p. 86.

88. *Ibid.*, p. 94.

89. NSC-68, *FRUS*, 1950, I, p. 238, 237.

90. NSC-7, *FRUS*, 1950, I, p. 545.

91. NSC 20/4, *FRUS*, 1950, I, p. 663.

92. NSC-68, *FRUS*, 1959, I, p. 264, 249.

93. *Ibid.*, p. 246.

94. *Ibid.*, p. 288.

95. NSC 20/4, *FRUS*, 1948, I, p. 666.

96. Report on Soviet Intentions, Joint Intelligence Committee, American Embassy, Moscow, *FRUS*, 1948, I, p. 551.

97. NSC 20/2, *FRUS*, 1948, I, 619.

98. NSC 20/4, *FRUS*, 1948, I, p. 664.

99. Gaddis, p. 84.

100. Tonelson, p. 85.

101. NSC-68, *FRUS*, 1950, I, p. 246-247.

102. Melanson, p. 155.

103. NSC-68, *FRUS*, 1950, I, p. 248-49.

104. NSC-68, p. 249.

105. NSC-68, *FRUS*, 1950, I, p. 252.

106. *Ibid.*, p. 252.

107. *Ibid.*, 241.

108. *Ibid.*, p. 242.

109. NSC 20/2, *FRUS*, 1948, I, p. 610.

110. NSC 20/1, *FRUS, 1948*, I, p. 611.

111. NSC-68, *FRUS*, 1950, I, p. 241.

112. *Ibid.*, p. 240.

113. *Ibid.*, p. 237-38.

114. NSC 20/4, *FRUS*, 1948, I, p. 665.

115. NSC-68, *FRUS*, 1959, I, p. 253, 255, 268.

116. NSC 20/2, *FRUS*, 1948, I, p. 617.

117. "Measures Required to Achieve U.S. Objectives with Respect to the U.S.S.R.," *FRUS*, 1949, I, 271-72.

118. NSC-68, *FRUS*, 1950, I, p. 276.

119. Gaddis, p. 104.

BIBLIOGRAPHY

Acheson, Dean. *Present at the Creation*, New York: W.W. Norton and Company, 1969.

Gaddis, John Lewis. *Strategies of Containment*, New York: Oxford University Press, 1982.

Hammond, Paul Y. "NSC-68: Prologue to Rearmament," in *Strategy, Politics and Defense Budgets*, edited by Warner Schilling, Hammond, and Glen R. Snyder, New York: Columbia University Press, 1962.

Hodgson, Godfrey. "The Establishment," *Foreign Policy*, num. 10, Spring 1973, pp. 3-40.

Johnston, Whittle. "The Containment of John Gaddis," *The National Interest*, Winter 1986/7, pp. 85-94.

Kaplan, Fred M. "Our Cold War Policy, Circa '50," *New York Times Magazine*, May 18, 1980.

Kennan, George F. *Memoirs 1925-1950*, Boston: Little, Brown and Company, 1967.

__________. "Sources of Soviet Conduct," *Foreign Affairs*, (25), 4, July 1946, pp. 566-82.

Melanson, Richard A. "Paul H. Nitze to Norman Podheretz: the Tradition of Anti-Communist Containment," in *Traditions and Values: American Diplomacy 1945 to Present*, Lanham, MD: University Press of America, 1984.

New York Times.

Nitze, Paul H. "The Development of NSC-68," *International Security*, (4) 4, Spring 1980, pp. 179-176.

________________ "Role of the Learned Man in Government," *Review of Politics*, (20), 3, July 1958.

Smith, Gaddis. *Dean Acheson*, in the series on *The American Secretaries of State and Their Diplomacy*, vol. xvi, edited by Robert H. Ferrell, New York: Cooper Square Publishers, 1972.

Theoharis, Alan. "The Rhetoric of Politics," in *Politics and Policies of the Truman Administration*, edited by Barton J. Bernstein, Chicago: Quadrangle Books, 1970.

Tonelson, Alan. "Nitze's World," *Foreign Policy*, number 35, Summer 1979, pp. 74-90.

United States Congress. Senate. Committee on Foreign Affairs. [Hearings in Executive Session] *Reviews of the World Situation, 1949-1950*, Washington, 1974.

United States Department of State. *Department of State Bulletin*, 1950.

________________. *Foreign Relations of the United States*, 1948, 1949, 1950.

Wells, Samuel. "Sounding the Tocsin," *International Security*, (4), 2, Fall 1979, pp. 116-158.

CHAPTER FOUR

Arms Control, Disarmament and the United Nations

WILLIAM EPSTEIN

NARRATOR: Although we've had a series of discussions on arms control, we have had no discussions on the role of the United Nations. It seemed logical, therefore, to bring the person who knows the most about the role of the U.N. and disarmament into our discussions.

William Epstein was one of the founding fathers of the United Nations. He has served the United Nations in one capacity or another for forty-two years. In the beginning he was the director of the disarmament division of the United Nations. He is and continues to be a senior special fellow at UNITAR (United Nations Institute for Training and Research). Mr. Epstein was born in Calgary, Canada. He practiced law before World War II; he served in the office of the agent of attorney general in Canada. He was educated at the London School of Economics in International Relations and at the University of Alberta in both arts and sciences and law, graduating in both instances with first-class honors, and other awards in legal studies. He was a senior Canadian member of the U.N. Secretariat for many years appointed to that Secretariat in 1946. He chaired the U.N. Staff Committee from 1949 to 1950 and then became director of the Disarmament Division in 1950 and chief of the disarmament group serving until 1972. He was chief and acting chief of the Middle East section of the Political and Security Council Affairs Department at the U.N. He was a member of the international group of experts that prepared the report on a comprehensive nuclear test ban treaty for the U.N. in 1980. He was chairman of the international group of consultant experts who prepared the report on chemical and biological weapons for the United Nations in the late 1960s. He represented the U.N. Secretary General at the Conference of Eighteen Nations Commission on Disarmament and the Conference of the Commission on Disarmament at Geneva in the decades of the 1960s and 1970s. The work of that group led to the Test Ban Treaty of 1963, the Nonproliferation Treaty of 1968, the Seabed Arms Control Treaty of 1968; and the Biological Weapons Convention of 1972.

Mr. Epstein also has had wide academic experience teaching at Carlton University in Ottawa; the University of California; as Regents Professor at the University of Calgary; the University of Victoria; the University of British Columbia, and many U.S. universities. He is the author of *The Last Chance: Nuclear Proliferation and Arms Control; New Directions in Disarmament; A New Design for Disarmament; The Prevention of Nuclear War: A United Nations Perspective; Twenty-Five Years of Effort* and *Disarmament, 1945-1970.*

When I worked in New York the watchword was that if you wanted to know anything about the role of the U.N. in disarmament, the person to ask was Bill Epstein. We've asked him, and despite inclement weather, he has come to Charlottesville. We are delighted that he is willing to join in our arms control series.

MR. EPSTEIN: Thank you very much, Kenneth Thompson. It is true and I'm very proud of the fact that I've been at the U.N. from the beginning and in disarmament for some forty odd years, even though some of my friends take delight in pointing out that I've spent all my adult life as a failure. But I think we are on the verge of maybe some new thinking on the world that's good for the U.N. and good for the world. I'm a bit of a missionary at heart for internationalism, multilateralism, and peace, and this gives me a good opportunity. The U.N. Charter which we could never get adopted in as good a form as it was in 1945 and 1946, is still a very extraordinary document. Its main purpose, of course, is to maintain international peace and security by means of collective security. It sets out a very comprehensive system, the most complete ever outlined for an international organization in history. I'll just list quickly what the main points are.

Firstly, the peaceful settlement of disputes, known as "peacemaking."

Secondly, enforcement measures against breaches of the peace or aggression, now called "peacekeeping." Those days it was called an "international police force" because under Article 43 military forces were to be placed at the disposal of the Security Council, but that never did get off the ground because of the Cold War.

Third is disarmament, but there is less emphasis in the Charter of the United Nations on disarmament and the regulation of arms than there was in the League of Nations Covenant, which had several lengthy articles. Here it is only mentioned rather casually in two or three articles of the charter. One reason for neglect of disarmament in the Charter is that all military forces were to be put at the disposal of the Security Council and the international police force, which of course never happened.

Fourth are economic and social progress. There has been more work done than is realized in the U.N. in that field directed toward economic development and human rights, particularly in the human rights. The progress made in international organization and international institutions, international law and human rights is something unique in modern history.

In decolonization, some people say we have had much success. We are responsible for over one hundred countries becoming independent. In almost all cases the United Nations started bringing countries to freedom and self-determination, not in all, but in nearly all cases, by peaceful means without bloodshed; that wasn't the rule before the United Nations.

Finally, the last principle is justice under international law which is still the objective. It has been weakened recently, mainly because of the United States not being willing to accept the compulsory jurisdiction of the International Court of Justice. But maybe that will change too.

The Charter was found fully adequate to prevent war, including nuclear war, although it was signed a few weeks before the nuclear bomb was exploded. The failure to implement it was due to the Cold War. Competition and rivalry between the United States and the Soviet Union was evident at the first meetings of the Security Council in 1946 in London. No forces were made available to the Security Council and it was left to Lester Pearson to devise an alternative. He invented the idea of peacekeeping forces, which could only operate with the consent of the parties in conflict but not wage war to fill the gap. They would be a buffer between hostile states in order to preserve the peace until the U.N. could bring about peaceful settlements. Because it wasn't working, because the U.N. international police forces, as they called them, failed in making forces available to the Security Council, the western powers established NATO as a partial collective security arrangement and the Soviet bloc set up the Warsaw Pact in response. In 1956 at the time of the Suez crisis, Pearson developed the idea of the U.N. peacekeeping forces for which he received the Nobel prize.

The United Nations, but not by itself, has been an important factor in preventing war involving the two superpowers arrayed against each other. Certainly the fear of the atomic bomb and later the hydrogen bomb played a role, but so did the very existence of this organization where a dialogue could continually go on with communication between the superpowers. Certainly our peacekeeping efforts have helped to limit, reduce and prevent the extension of some of the wars in the Third World. It has helped to keep things from getting out of hand. Superpower relations have been stabilized on the whole in the postwar world, despite periods of tension and a few crises like the Cuban missile crisis and the Berlin crisis. There has been relative stability. There are some 160 independent nations in the world today; at the time of the League of Nations there were only some forty. It is not surprising that there are conflicts every once in a while, but except for two or three big ones—Vietnam, Korea, Afghanistan and to some extent Iran-Iraq—the U.N. has managed to prevent the others from getting out of hand.

As one American once said to me, "All of the monies that we paid to the U.N. are peanuts compared with what we would have had to pay if there were not the U.N.

peacekeeping forces in the Middle East." During all those years, during the Cold War and in good times and bad times, there was always a continuous discussion and dialogue. It may at times have been a dialogue of the deaf, but nevertheless the U.N. has provided a means of communication between east and west, between the two superpowers.

Disarmament was probably the main continuous subject of debate between them. I use the expression "disarmament," which is the United Nations generic expression that covers everything from confidence-building measures to general and complete disarmament. It is a generic term but the Americans invented the term "arms control" in the 1950s, which is a sort of modernized version of what used to be known, at the time of League of Nations, as arms "regulation."

In the first ten years of the U.N. because of the A-bomb and nuclear weapons, it was good that they had this ability to discuss things because nobody understood very much about this terrible new weapon. The Cold War had frozen all of the enforcement measures and had also frozen our peacemaking capabilities. Nevertheless, the mere fact that there was this dialogue, which did manage to keep a measure of stability, enabled both superpowers to take their measure of the other. Each one was putting forward ideas that they knew the other couldn't ever accept. But each one in putting forward those ideas was outlining its main concerns and letting the other side know its position, and that gave them some idea where the boundary beyond which neither one of them could go was.

Then a tremendous change took place in the U.N. In the early days every resolution was adopted by more or less forty-five to five with three abstentions. The majority included the United States and the western powers; the minority was the Soviet Union and its two or three allies. The non-aligned included the three leading neutralist countries in the world in those days: India, Egypt and Indonesia. Because of the tremendous upsurge in decolonization or anticolonialism, it was important that the U.N. help to channel and regulate it and see that it went smoothly.

The smaller powers now are by far the majority out of the one hundred and fifty-nine members of the U.N. Today the smaller powers can count about 115 or 120 votes, so they can get the two-thirds majority in anything they want. They are nearly all developing Third World countries, at least the smaller ones are. In fact, a wisecrack against the U.N. is that "the trouble with the U.N. is that the smaller countries run it." The Secretary General's answer to that is "that's true, they do run the U.N. from Forty-second Street to Forty-eight Street from First Avenue to the East River. The rest of the world is run by the big powers, the superpowers." That is still true. One of the reasons why the present administration got tough, and the Congress got even tougher, is because of this shift in voting power. Even when the Soviet Union, the United States and their respective allies vote together, they can't get a two-thirds majority on anything. The only bloc who can command a two-thirds majority is the developing states. That is a problem that we haven't entirely worked out, although I think it is on the road to being reconciled.

One of the things that disenchanted the American people in government—in fact Reagan mentioned it in his last speech in September, 1987 to the United Nations—was that terrible resolution that proclaimed that "Zionism is racism." That did more to turn off American support for the U.N. than any other single thing. Another thing which turns them off is when people say that the little countries, the nonaligned countries or the Third World countries, are all anti-American. That's not true; they just put forward ideas that don't coincide with the American ideas of what they think should go on in the world. The Soviet Union was a little bit smarter than the Americans. Instead of pushing their own ideas all the time, which never got them anywhere, they have joined the nonaligned bandwagon and they support them in their votes. It seems to the United States that the U.N. has become anti-American, which it is not. Certainly the United States is on the short end and almost isolated in many of the votes. They are beginning to change that now; they are beginning once again to be active in putting forward resolutions and looking for consensus or large-scale support. That seems to be going on.

To turn to what has happened to disarmament and the hopes for achievements in negotiations running from disarmament to arms control, a tendency exists in periods of increasing tension to observe that we make no headway in many fields and no agreements whatsoever in disarmament. During periods of detente or the relaxation of tension, however, we do negotiate all sorts of agreements in many fields, but this is particularly noticeable in the field of arms control and disarmament.

For example, during the first fifteen years of the Cold War at the United Nations, there were volumes that would fill this room on the debates and discussion of disarmament, but there was no agreement. After the Cuban missile crisis when both powers had looked down into the abyss and stepped back, they started talking more seriously about disarmament. The 1960s and 1970s were golden years. In those years, we achieved some nine or ten multilateral treaties including the Helsinki Pact, which was a multilateral treaty. Some of the agreements were important. We had the partial test ban treaty, the nonproliferation treaty, the biological weapons convention, as well as thirteen bilateral Soviet-American treaties, starting with the hot line and the partial test ban treaty, which started out as a trilateral agreement. There followed the SALT I and SALT II agreements, and some of the things that have gone on in between. The high water mark of our progress was in 1978 at the first U.N. Special Session on Disarmament, where the lead was taken by the nonaligned countries. They worked hard on both the Americans and the Russians, and they came up with what is called the final document of the first Special Session adopted by consensus. You couldn't get it today, but you could reluctantly get it then and it is still a sort of bible for progress in arms control and disarmament.

That was the end of the period, the last act of the period of detente because in 1979 there was the invasion of Afghanistan and the withdrawal of the SALT II Treaty, which probably couldn't have passed the Senate. There have been no agreements whatsoever during the Reagan years which have been the years of chill except when things began to ease slightly with the Stockholm Agreement for confidence-building and security-building measures in Europe.

Despite those twenty-odd agreements, there has been no reversal and no halt in the arms race, particularly the nuclear arms race. In fact the arms race is proceeding at a faster pace today than ever before in history. Military expenditures are a measure of how it is proceeding, especially global military spending. In 1959 we spent about $100 billion a year, and now about $1 trillion a year. That's more than a $100 million every hour. My brain is not capable of encompassing how much money that is, but obviously it's a wasteful expenditure because it doesn't produce producer goods or consumer goods. It doesn't provide you with food, clothing or shelter. It is supposed to provide you with security, but you are spending an awful lot more money for that; it's no wonder the world is in an economic mess, as it really is. When the world is wasting that much money on armaments, it is better to junk them than to use them, or sell them or give them away to the poor countries that don't need them. Indeed they need them less.

I would propose another measure. In 1969 when SALT negotiations first began with Nixon and Kissinger, and Brezhnev and Gromyko, the U.S. then had some 1,700 strategic warheads. It now has about 12,000. The U.S.S.R. had twelve hundred strategic warheads and now has around 11,000. Between the two of them, the superpowers have close to 50,000 nuclear weapons, 95 percent of all existing nuclear weapons in the world. To call this overkill is really an understatement. It is absolute madness. There is no way in the world you can use that many. There are only about 200 major cities with a population over 100,000 to 150,000 each in the United States and the Soviet Union. This constant build-up of more and more killing power is something I've never been able to understand. It is not only obscene and indecent; it is immoral because of what it takes away from the fulfillment of human needs.

In the SALT agreements Brezhnev, Nixon and later Carter tried to limit the nuclear arms race in numbers, quantitatively. Qualitatively, it became more dangerous than ever because of the rapid pace of advancing technology. The development of accuracy in nuclear missiles became the real enemy because people got the notion that the weapons are so accurate they could knock out the other side's missiles. With the first strike, you could knock them out before they could retaliate, which is nonsense because you can't detect, locate and knock out their submarines. Each side has more than enough submarine launched ballistic missiles (SLBMs) to completely destroy the other country.

In fact, President Carter in his State of the Union address in 1979 pointed out that the captain of one Poseidon submarine, which had a 116 missiles with 10 warheads each, could destroy the Soviet Union as a functioning entity. If that is true, and the United States at that time had the thirty-one Poseidons and ten Polaris's, now they are building Tridents which are much more powerful, with longer range and greater accuracy. It is incomprehensible to me why any rational people would have to keep up this huge build-up instead of building down their arsenals. They have more than could conceivably be used if civilization and humanity are to survive.

Then the U.S. started to produce weapons quantitatively. SALT II never was ratified, mainly but not solely because of Afghanistan. For years, conservatives had been screaming that the Soviet Union was catching up and getting ahead. When President Reagan and Secretary of Defense Weinberger came in, they started talking about a limited nuclear war and fighting, prevailing and winning a protracted nuclear war. The Pentagon Guidance Plan says that "even though"—they changed the language—they couldn't win a nuclear war, they could "prevail in a protracted nuclear war" which means the same thing. Each side was busy in a competition to gain superiority over the other, although Kissinger said when he came back from the Vladivostok summit meeting with President Ford that depending on ever larger numbers of weapons was absurd. He asked, what does superiority mean in a nuclear age when each side can completely destroy the other, no matter who strikes first. How do you know you have it? What do you do with it if you do have it? All these were very sound questions. In his farewell address President Eisenhower put his finger on the real problem, which everybody remembers as "the military-industrial complex." Very few people remember that he also warned against the military bureaucratic complex in the Soviet Union, which is the same thing.

In this period of Cold War the Soviet Union couldn't match the dynamism of the rather elderly President Reagan because they had Brezhnev, Andropov and Chernenko, all of whom were old and ill and not doing well. So things went badly.

The United States, I think, has a love affair with deterrence, all except Reagan; he certainly hasn't. Every new weapon, even those that are clearly intended for a first strike and don't really affect the nuclear balance at all, is justified as enhancing deterrence. Nevertheless, the United States, although it says deterrence is its policy, reserves the right of first use of nuclear weapons, while China and the Soviet Union have unilaterally pledged never to be the first to use nuclear weapons. No first use is not what you would call a verifiable or an enforceable policy, but nevertheless it does affect the climate. The gang of four (George Kennan, McGeorge Bundy, Gerard Smith and Robert McNamara) in a *Foreign Affairs* article also declare that first use of nuclear weapons would be madness."

Although the Soviet Union never acknowledged that they rely on deterrence and used different language, they still abide by that same policy.

I am one of those who thinks the idea of a nuclear war by intention or design is impossible. I don't think they are that crazy, either in Moscow or Washington. Each of us can name two or three crazies who lead Third World states whom we would not trust if they acquired nuclear weapons. I am one of those who have a gut feeling that if either Iraq or Iran had a nuclear bomb, they would have used it. Certainly Iraq has used chemical weapons against Iran.

But the danger is not just the proliferation of nuclear weapons to reckless leaders, but also of nuclear war by accident, miscalculation, or human or mechanical breakdown. They call it command, control, communications and intelligence, involving the escalation of some local conventional war or, God forbid, a limited nuclear war if nuclear weapons spread (and I am convinced they will). If the nuclear powers don't take the lead and do what they are committed to doing in several treaties, including the Nonproliferation Treaty, the nuclear arms race will continue.

Then too you can't exclude the possibility of the crazies acquiring the weapons. Gadhafi tried very hard, and so has Iran off and on, to acquire nuclear weapons. Fortunately they haven't succeeded. But if this thing goes on, then we'll get nuclear terrorism, not just state terrorism but terrorism by subnational groups.

This whole idea of deterrence has certainly played some sort of a role. Nobody can document how much of a role it has played, but it has certainly played a role through the balance of power or balance of terror in preventing a nuclear war between the superpowers. Still, there is no guarantee it is going to hold forever. It reminds me of the story of a man falling off a skyscraper and, after he passes the fortieth story, he says to himself, "So far so good." That's about the situation we are in with the escalating arms race and the philosophy of deterrence.

Given that I'm not a great admirer of the policies of President Reagan, I will say this for Reagan. In his third month in office he sent out word that he wanted to know how to get rid of nuclear weapons. He sent out a memo to people to respond. Unfortunately a man named Edward Teller got to him and sold him on the idea of "Star Wars," or SDI. In March 1983 he talked about making nuclear weapons "impotent and obsolete" and that was the beginning of SDI. At least he was motivated by the idea that we have to get rid of the nuclear threat. I don't think he chose the right way, because I think SDI isn't going to make nuclear weapons impotent or obsolete. Certainly no scientist I know would say that it can really protect populations in cities, but a number of them do think it will be successful in the defense of silos. Nobody knows how successful, though. I am convinced that it will not get rid of nuclear weapons or deterrence, because I think it will lead to a triple arms race: first, for defensive weapons; second, for continuing offensive weapons in order to be able to survive defensive weapons attack; and third, for a race in countermeasures in order to overcome SDI. I don't think that's the way to do it, but nevertheless Reagan was motivated by the right idea.

One thing that may have been a positive result of SDI, it has clearly scared the Soviet military and political leaders, because even though their advisers tell them it can't work, they cannot give them any assurance that it won't work. After all many people, Rutherford among others, said, "It is nonsense to think that you could ever have an atomic bomb." You never know what can work. It will mean that the Soviets are going to have to work on SDI and "Star Wars," and they are going to have to keep their offensive weapons. As they have said time and time again, "We cannot afford to give up our offensive weapons if you are going to go in for defensive weapons." They know that they can't keep up with American science and technology or military technology; they can't afford to try. I'm sure this country can't either, because nobody knows how many hundreds of billions of dollars it is going to cost to try to work out an effective SDI.

By one of these happy quirks of history, the three old Soviet leaders passed from the scene and a new, young dynamic man named Gorbachev rose to leadership in the Soviet Union late in 1985. At the risk of being misunderstood, I'll say he is undoubtedly the leading man of vision and courage on the international scene today. He understands that Soviet communism or socialism cannot survive without some new approach to international affairs and political and military thinking. He calls it "new thinking" or *glasnost*, which means more openness, because secrecy engenders fear, mistrust and lack of confidence; "perestroika," or the restructuring of their system, is required because their old system wasn't working. He has come up with an avalanche of new proposals and initiatives. It is difficult to keep up with him, even for those of us who spend our time doing it. He refuses to take "no" for an answer and keeps coming back to the United States with one new proposal after another. I'll quickly try to list some of them.

On January 15, 1986, he came out with a complete plan to eliminate all nuclear weapons in three stages by the year 2000 but it had to be on the basis that there would be no SDI, which of course the United States rejected.

Then he went to Reykjavik, one of the most unusual—some people described it weird—summit conferences ever to take place in modern times. In Geneva when the leaders met for the first time in November 1985, they both made public statements declaring that they subscribed to the idea that a nuclear war cannot be won and must never be fought. That was an important clarifying statement in itself. They also agreed that they would meet in 1986. Then they verbally agreed to rid the world of all nuclear weapons, though for different reasons and with different approaches. Reagan was still thinking of his SDI approach and Gorbachev was thinking of the Soviet's basic approach that you could rid the world of nuclear weapons. They agreed on that goal, but there was no agreement on how to achieve it. Nevertheless, it became the new point of departure for all subsequent negotiations which are going on at the present time.

Let's consider the idea that getting rid of all nuclear weapons has scared the U.S. allies. They became worried that if Europe didn't have nuclear weapons, they would be left with a marked inferiority in conventional weapons. Although some scholars say that certainly the Soviets have a superiority in number, it is highly dubious as to what extent that superiority makes up for the superior quality of the West's conventional weapons. Also there is no doubt that the western allies are a lot more dependable from the United States' point of view than are the eastern allies for the Soviet Union. I remember a Soviet colonel telling a Canadian colonel—I'm a Canadian still so I am free to criticize either the United States or Canada—"I don't know why you are so excited about our having 17,000 tanks, three times more than you. You people don't understand that we have to keep two or three tanks in every village in eastern Europe to help them celebrate their liberation." They have a sense of humor, at least. They aren't too sure that they can rely on their allies.

Now I will try to deal with a few of the main problems. It seems certain, as far as you can be to being certain about anything in international affairs, that we are going to have an INF Treaty signed by Gorbachev and Reagan with double zero—zero intermediate range nuclear weapons with 600 to 3,000 miles in range, and zero with shorter range ones 300 to 600 miles. In Europe and Asia the intermediate range weapons are going to be totally eliminated, and in Europe they are going to eliminate all of the shorter range ones.

The NATO Nuclear Planning Committee, despite all misgivings and its fears for Europe, unanimously agreed to support the agreement. But this agreement will have very little military significance. They are going to reduce some 400 of the U.S. weapons in the intermediate range field and also the shorter range field, and some 1,600 Soviet weapons—some 2,000 weapons in all. Yet this is only 3-5 percent of the total stockpiles that the two powers have. It will have little military significance because all of the strategic weapons—the intercontinental ballistic missiles, the submarine launched missiles, and the bombers—are still going to remain. They are the real basis of deterrence. Also they are still going to have submarine, surface vessels and planes and each is going to have about 5,000 short range battlefield or tactical nuclear weapons up to a range of 300 miles. They are the most dangerous of all. We should get rid of those immediately because, if there is even a minor outbreak and one side is about to be overrun, the combatants are going to use them or lose them. They really are no good at all; they could result in the destruction of a large part of Europe simply because they exist.

But the INF agreement does have a tremendous political and psychological significance. This is the first nuclear weapons treaty after more than seventeen years and, as both sides keep on reiterating, it is also the first treaty to get rid of a whole category of nuclear weapons. Most important of all, it could be the beginning of a new process for arms control and disarmament and the beginning of a new era. If "detente" is a dirty word, it does mean better relations between the superpowers.

Then we come to the hard problem of the next step, the reduction of strategic weapons. Here the problem is, how long will the ABM Treaty be observed and will it be observed under the narrow or the broad interpretation? In other words, how fast can the United States go forward with SDI? They agreed at Reykjavik to 50 percent reductions in five years and 100 percent reductions (this was an agreement in principle) of all ballistic missiles within ten years. Gorbachev on January 16, 1988, at Reykjavik said, "Let's get rid of all nuclear weapons in ten years." The United States wouldn't agree to that.

Despite differences, they did agree that they would also discuss the observance of and nonwithdrawal from the ABM Treaty for an agreed period, but they haven't resolved their differences or whether it will be the narrow interpretation, which means no testing and deployment in outer space, or the broad interpretation. The Soviet Union has made concession after concession. They hold to a very narrow interpretation. They said testing only inside laboratories, then testing on land, but none in outer space. The United States has said, "No, under the broad interpretation of the ABM Treaty we can test in space too. The only thing that is banned is deployment." But that view is not universally held.

The only question that remains is whether there is some room for compromise. The Soviet Union did propose that we get our military people together to discuss what kind of testing is permissible. The United States said "no." There are hints of additional flexibility on both sides, and if they can agree on an interpretation of the ABM Treaty, what parts and how it could be observed, then there is room for progress toward a 50 percent reduction. Some people are hoping that when Reagan goes to Moscow in May 1988, the leaders will conclude a treaty on strategic missiles.

On the nuclear test ban, some say the Soviet Union sold the store to the United States in the agreement of 17 September 1987, because they wanted a nuclear test ban, which they are committed to legally and in every other way under the Partial Test Ban Treaty of 1963 and the Nonproliferation Treaty of 1968. The American position has been that they are now only interested in the test ban as a long-term goal as part of the process of getting rid of all nuclear weapons.

There was an article in the *New York Times* that argued we could get rid of them sometime in the twenty-first century. The Soviet Union finally agreed to a step-by-step negotiation that will begin by the first of December, 1988. In the announcement to the United Nations, the negotiators said that they want to limit each side to four tests a year, not exceeding one kiloton in yield. The Americans aren't going to agree to that, so I don't expect much progress there, which is a shame because, unless you can stop testing and developing qualitatively, the technological arms race will continue. If you cut by 50 percent, you have deep cuts, but if you replace all the weapons with more modernized and dangerous ones, you are not that much farther ahead even if the numbers are reduced. We have to have a nuclear test ban forever to halt the nuclear arms race.

To conclude, I do want to say something about the role of the U.N. There are differences and, surprisingly, a few similarities in Gorbachev's and Reagan's styles and approaches. But at the U.N., the growing complexity of the problems confronting the nations of the world is becoming more and more evident. Every major problem is a global one with a multilateral dimension. Consider poverty, population and pollution. They are all interrelated and they apply all over the world, as do disarmament, development and international security. Not only are all nations now interdependent, but all these issues are interlinked, and they can only be dealt with effectively, not on a national or a bilateral basis, but only on a global or international basis. This requires international cooperation, international law and international organization. If the U.N. did not exist today, we'd have to go out and invent it.

There is no such thing anymore as national security without international security. The security of the Soviet Union and the United States depends on the degree and the extent to which they can convince each other that their security must be assured. That is the key. If the Soviet Union cannot convince the United States that its security is assured and the United States cannot convince the Soviet Union its security is assured, there is no way we are going to have a disarmed or a more peaceful, less militarized world.

In the last decade, this whole concept of multilateralism—and I regret to say this is due to a large extent due to the Reagan administration—has been challenged. It has come under direct attack and there has been a greater move toward unilateralism in international relations. The Secretary General of the United Nations has felt constrained to warn a couple of years ago that the world was "perilously near a new international anarchy because of the erosion of the status and authority of international institutions." Fortunately, in the last year or two wiser counsel has begun to prevail. All of the nations of the world, but in particular and most importantly nuclear powers and the five permanent members of the Security Council, including the two superpowers, are rediscovering the indispensability of the United Nations. It is the sole body that can grapple with global problems and provide a constant and ready mechanism for collective action.

Somebody said that it was man's ability to act rationally that made the United Nations possible, but it is man's capacity to act irrationally that makes it absolutely necessary. They are beginning to understand this. In fact, more and more voices are heard that the best way to deal, even with Iran or Iraq in the Gulf crisis, is to let the U.N. do it, as with peacekeeping forces in the Middle East and in Cyprus. We've had at least a dozen successful experiences with U.N. peacekeeping operations.

In this nuclear age when each superpower can absolutely destroy the world, when there is the threat of nuclear terrorism and ordinary terrorism, when there is the illegal drug problem, when there is the AIDS epidemic, any one of these problems can undermine our civilization and the entire world community. Such issues can only be successfully addressed and dealt with on an international basis. The nations of the world are beginning to recognize that they must be dealt with as a result of international cooperation and international action. In this respect, the role of the public is decisive. The public in all countries have to persuade their governments that it is time for all of them to engage in a new way of thinking if they want this world to survive. We in the U.N. are tremendously encouraged—I won't go into the details of it—by the new Soviet comprehensive system of international security. Gorbachev outlined it all on September 19, 1987, in the Soviet press, and it has been published in English. It offers innumerable new initiatives and suggestions. They are not all going to work, but they are going to result in a whole new approach to the question of international security.

The idea of the world community and world organization has not been tried and found wanting. The idea of the world community and the world organization has not been put to an effective test or tried seriously. Now we are on the threshold of such a thing. The Soviet Union is going all the way and there are encouraging signs of that in this country too. Most of the hard-line conservatives have begun to leave the government, and there is evidence that the people of this country want a change from the old rivalry and confrontation. If the people press hard enough for it, I think we have a good chance of surviving.

QUESTION: Eliot Richardson and Cyrus Vance have both been saying that the U.N. peacekeeping force should be used in the Persian Gulf. Why does the U.S. insist on going it alone in the Gulf?

MR. EPSTEIN: Because they think that they can keep better control and keep the Russians out without one. That's the answer.

QUESTION: Aren't the reasons the United States feels that it has to act alone been because the Soviet Union refuses to accept any inspection of their arsenals?

MR. EPSTEIN: There are new things that are developing here too. I didn't outline the difference between Gorbachev and Reagan, but the Soviet Union has now offered many kinds of verification, including on-site inspection. In fact, on the Chemical Treaty and on one or two other treaties, they've offered more verification than the United States will accept. So there is new thinking going on in the Soviet Union. Obviously they are seeking the high ground for good public relations, but nevertheless there are things going on.

They've even announced they are going to have a conference next year on human rights in the Soviet Union, an international conference. There are also the beginnings of limited elections in the communist system. Gorbachev has announced they are going to give more autonomy to their allies in eastern Europe. They are not going to insist that they follow them slavishly. I think the important thing is to start taking advantage of these changes. You don't have to accept them as gospel, but by all means let's get into a discussion about them.

COMMENT: Regarding Gorbachev's personality, an interesting bit of information surfaced recently. One of his close associates and friends while he was attending Moscow University was a Czech communist by the name of Stenek Mlynar, who is now a dissident living in exile in Vienna. It shows that Gorbachev's thinking was shaped by other people along the way as he was coming up. I am somewhat familiar with the Czech scene, having been a Fellow there for a year. This is a good omen.

MR. EPSTEIN: I, too, have had experience with two of his advisers. Anatoly Dobrynin, who was the dean of the diplomatic corps in Washington for a long time, was an undersecretary general of the United Nations in the political department and I was a director under him. Even in those days we found him an unusual Russian. You could argue and discuss issues with him. The man who has even exceeded Dobrynin is Alexander Yakalov, for ten years the Soviet ambassador in Canada. He was out of favor for a time because his ideas were a little bit too radical for the Brezhnev period, but he has now been brought back to the Soviet Union. He is a member of the Politburo in charge of ideology. I know this man personally because he is head of the Canadian Pugwash group. We invited him to come and speak to us at the twenty-fifth anniversary of the Pugwash movement in Pugwash, Nova Scotia in 1982, and again he expressed rather forward looking ideas. Velakov, who is vice president of their Academy of Sciences, is a scientist who has been involved in Pugwash. He is practically bristling with all sorts of new ideas. With these people playing the important role, there is a lot in the new thinking in *glasnost* and *perestroika* and the desire for democratization.

NARRATOR: I'm sure I speak for all of you in thanking Mr. Epstein for coming here on a day like this. Bill Epstein has had long years of public service. We have a number of people who are just beginning who have all the advantages of youth and energy. It would be difficult to imagine, however, anybody bringing the same enthusiasm, dedication, and commitment to international efforts. Ten years from now, when we have him back, you will see that he has retained the same energy and the same commitment. It has been a pleasure to have him at Virginia.

Concluding Observations

As is true of most books or essays, this little volume is an introduction and not a definitive answer to the question "who decides?" It introduces some challenging and provocative approaches that may help citizens and students better understand who are the principal actors or who ought to be involved in arms control and national security. More than most volumes in the Miller Center's arms control series, the element of controversy is evident throughout this treatise. Some contributors maintain Congress should have a more clearly delineated role while others question whether Congress can negotiate. Others see the president as the main player. It is said by some that the present team of arms control negotiators in the Reagan administration is strong and sufficient to their task but others question whether it can continue to meet the challenge. In any administration, certain public servants play a critical role.

A book of this kind with contributors addressing different aspects of the arms control problem plainly cannot give an incoming administration or its negotiators a guidebook for action. Nor can it tell a president to whom he should turn as principal negotiators or which arena or institution is best suited for discussion. What it does provide is a relatively concise review of some of the main issues to consider in approaching the overarching question "who decides?" In this important respect, it may help others who at some future time may deal with arms control to face choices and decisions in this vital sphere of foreign policy. It may also lead future thinkers to continue the discussion to which the authors of the present essays contribute. These papers are, at the very least, the beginning of a most important inquiry likely to go on for decades into the future as we seek to determine "who decides."

eightpale**women**

eight pale women

women pale

james c. hopkins

THE WORD WORKS
CAPITAL COLLECTION
WASHINGTON, D.C.

First Edition
First Printing
eight pale women
Copyright © 2003 by James C. Hopkins

The WORD WORKS
PO Box 42164
Washington, DC 20015
editor@wordworksdc.com

Cover photograph: James C. Hopkins

Book design, typography by Janice Olson

Library of Congress Number: 2002115064
International Standard Book Number: 0-915380-53-6

acknowledgments

the following poems have appeared, sometimes in an earlier version, in the following journals and anthologies:

journals

Carriage House Review
le cadavre exquis at the villa la rocca

The Federal Poet
cakewalk • balance and the nitro house
• the walnut tree waits for its bees

Frantic Egg
waking in a basement on the first day of spring

Love's Chance
pomegranate

Minimus
francis the diving mule • a morning like this

WordWrights!
black octopus • eight pale women

anthologies

Cabin Fever: Poets at the Joaquin Miller Cabin
the devil beating his wife

A Gradual Twilight: An Appreciation of John Haines
self-portrait

Winners: A Retrospective of the Washington Prize
finding my way (published as lumbini, nepal)

table of contents

f o u r

for marni

one

one chance

snow-
white birds
under
blackberry bushes.

in a
foreign country
spring
came twice,
and a
half-moon
broke
the clouds.

at night,
a man
taps softly
on a
wooden
door.

self-portrait

fifty miles north of fairbanks
the asphalt gives out
the gravel begins
and there's six hundred miles to go.

here's where you start to see yourself from above—
tiny red pickup in a sea of fir,
the upper left corner of the world.

and a hundred miles later
it's the arctic circle
and even the a.m. radio dies.
only satellites peeking out from the lid of the sky.

and then wide-eyed but groggy at 1 a.m.
you slog into coldfoot for gas—
brand new boots ankle-deep in mud
as soon as you jump from the cab.

grilled cheese for 5 bucks
in a room full of stares,
a jack london paperback safe and dry
inside your gore-tex jacket.

here the red-eyed waitress
hates them bastards in washington,
will never go back to america
she swears.

by 3 a.m.
the road straightens out—
the dodge casting shadows
but the headlights still on bright.

here's where you wonder
about tire irons and water,
blink back grizzly and caribou,
sing crazy about summer.

a few fir trees scraping antlers and fish full of river,
whole mountains like dogs
howling at the light.

and no sound but the truck
fighting through gravel—
an eye opening up for you
ghosting through night.

then here's where you stop
at the edge of the tundra.
the engine still running,
the door open wide.

you're outside in the cold
blowing on fingers,
setting camera on granite
with its tiny red light.

you've taken off running
like some drunken astronaut,
rising and sinking
across the mossy planet.

running and falling,
and running and falling.
waiting for something,
like the whole thing, to blink.

death of a skydiver

breathe out,
it's alright.
exhale blue and
the sky will rise and spread,
filling with flashes of silver planes
that circle overhead like angels.
loosen your grip on the cords
and let go the cloth in your hand—
the nylon cloud, orange and yellow,
that falls across your face like a shroud.
let the clouds drift over your lips,
shading the light from your eyes.
let the hot thistle of sun
roll across your tongue and return
to its place in the sky—
the sky that you came
screaming through,
planting yourself
like a blazing flower
in the open palm
of the earth.

reasons

a stalled car
simmering
in the mohave.

sagebrush
and obsolete
ochre mountains.

a soapgold smear
of some borrowed
clouds.

and the
far-off wingflap
of india.

i am falling
from my family
like a stone.

leaving

i'm three days
and many trains awake.
in a faux-marble walk-up
off the main bazaar.
ceiling fan stirring
the mosquito air,
locomotive pound and shriek below—
calcutta baking at dawn.

you lie
in our sweat
beneath mosquito netting,
check my breathing
and believe
i'm still sleeping,
then slip out quiet
into sticky flip-flops,
padding to the shower
down the hall.

leaving me
finally
beneath this white veil-swirl—
with its tiny holes
that keep out the wingings,
the things that prick
against the skin.
thin flutter and again,
alone at last.

incense and babble,
stomping in the hall,

dogs and iron on my tongue.
stretched to the edges
of a filthy bed,
against an instant
drawn out clear and cold—
i'm ready to arch us
into loneliness.

then i'm backpacked, moving
without closing the door,
two-stair skipping
cheating the desk
down and out
into the crumbling station
and a first-class sleeper
to benares.

vast on the platform
begs tattered india—
rafters aflap with pigeon settle,
its lepers, fingerless,
cupping the wind.

they chant up god
into silver bowls.
(on my shirt
a strand of your hair).
they lift up
ragged on cotton wings,
bathing
in shimmering air.

boy on the train platform in calcutta

he sees me at the other end, through the mass of people
and, of course, i'm horrified, then heart racing,
panicked, by the sureness that he's coming
my way, scraping those swollen dusty
things not-feet and pushing them
ahead with a leathery swoosh
past the heads now turning
to watch a new show—
and i've never really
seen it, so i can't
look away or
stop the
smile
blooming
across his face
or the small voice
saying, "elephant feet,"
so clearly, as though he's
teaching me a new language,
a new word that might describe
how a tall, pale man near the edge
of the world might set down his suitcase,
remove the veil that keeps him from the light,
and creep out of his skin into the sweating crowd,
pushing his past before him like so much unneeded flesh.

lumbini, nepal

—birthplace of the buddha

twelve-hour bus clatter across the terai,
a few stops for chai, chapati and daal.
i'm wedged in beside a chattering nepali doctor
in a red sari-swirl of exhaust, sweat and dust.

at the edge of town we squeal to a stop.
i unfold, descend to the middle of the road.
dustcloud, heat, faces pressed to the glass.
rustling bodhi leaves. the silence of alone.

the sly village innkeeper leads me upstairs
to a rooftop room worth a full month's pay.
poster eyes of the buddha above the doorway.
wind sifting the fields below.

the scratch of a match on the box's edge.
the splash of flame against the walls.
slow sandalwood curling of smoke into air.
far from familiar, i breathe in home.

how may we be of kind helping, sir?

two waiters with eyes full of menace and opium
the maitre d' in his apron and a stuttering busboy
all hovering like fish at the edge of my table.
i'm the only patron in the only restaurant, far from town.

i lift my fork. they whisper and twitch.
i set it down. and they bring me another.
suddenly lights go out and it's utterly black.
in just one week, though, i've learned not to panic.

breathe in the darkness. breathe out again.
basmati rice and incense, cardamom and kerosene.
the generator sputters and rumbles out back
and the manic maitre d' scrambles for candles.

the lime-green walls are fluttering back into sight,
the fish are schooling and gliding back in,
but i'm up and moving, rupees left on the plate,
already heading for the road, escaping into night.

finding my way

my sandaled feet on a road of hand-crushed stone
and a candle that lights only the next six steps.
i'm moving towards bed, and peace at last,
in the simplicity of an immense and foreign night.

through fields of grasses that whisper out on either side
remarking on nothing beneath a moonless sky.
past the sleeping watchman beneath his sacred trees—
sunrise hawker of incense, marigolds, and massage.

somewhere in this darkness lie a hundred more pilgrims
breathing starward behind monastery walls.
my footfalls in the dark. the backandforth bark of dogs.
prayer flags fluttering in the trees like ghosts.

tonight i am a circle of light on the road.
the language of movement and walking are the same.
here the only demons are the work of the mind
and longest journey is made outside of time.

two

night fishing

calm tonight.
and a light north wind
sets off the starboard beam.
it seems like years
we've been out here hunting,
chasing *spanish* through the black.
ploughing back and forth
beneath the tilted bears,
and following wherever the shadows lead—
weaving across the darkest water,
tilling our own wake into mounds.

back in the sound
you leave the lighthouse behind
but you're still within sight of the sweep.
the farther you go, the deeper you get.
you watch what you know
disappear to a point
until, finally, you're here—
you've lost the land completely,
and you're standing
with a knife in your hand.
the fish move ahead.
they cut to port through the black.
and even the beacon
can't get you back home.

calm tonight.
a little light from the moon.
the bears lie back in the water.
a man on the deck
with a squinting blade
holds a fish to his chest like a lover.
the breeze moves the hairs
on the back of his neck.
the moon glints cold off of its scales.
he cuts out the tongue
of the thrashing mackerel
and tosses it
into a pail.

summer sundays

grandpa loved a hand-cut hickory pipe
with a thick black stem.
some summer sundays
after god and cows had been tended,
after grandma had cleared the plates
for fourteen, fifteen, sixteen
daughters, granddaughters, grandsons
and after the pecan pie was served,
he'd tilt back from the table
suck in a healthy puff,
and say the words to
free the barefoot soul of every twelve-year-old
trapped in loafers and a clip-on tie—
"now who might be interested in ice cream?"

and we'd rush forward with a shout
to be chosen bucket-toter, ice-fetcher,
cream-carrier, salt-bearer, even peach-peeler.
just to be chosen at all
by the man with the hickory pipe
and the tanned tractor hands.
then to scatter full-tilt from the table
headlong through the kitchen
bursting onto the back porch
through a tangle of dogs
to launch from the cool of the house
into a blazing pinwheel of sun and summer grass,
before the screen door banged
and mama yelled something you couldn't quite make out.

later, with churn assembled and spinning
in its secret mix of salt and ice,
our lawn chairs circled and waiting,
we'd watch with wonder
his steady turning, turning, never-resting arm—
brown to the sleeve, milk white beneath,
plowing arm of any weather,
turning the groaning crank of a creaking barrel
as cream gave in to dasher.
then the magical moment
when the brown arm stopped,
and the lid was lifted,
and the cream
flashed cold and perfect.

now september,
 i stretch on a worn chaise lounge in a dusty lawn,
waiting for a breeze that i know will never come.
cicadas buzz in the mimosas he planted
and the old dog shifts and sighs.
i think of how we attacked that cold ice cream
not knowing until we'd finished
how hungry we'd really been.
at the end of the peach orchard
the dry leaves begin to touch and rustle.
the song of the cicadas rises from the higher branches,
and through it i hear the far-off ticking
of a tractor plowing the lowgrounds.
or the sound of a spoon scraping an empty bowl.

black octopus

on that july night,
when everything changed
we all tumbled
into the farm-use ford
with a learner's permit
and a case of bud
and wound out fifteen
mountain miles
to the fairfield firemen's carnival

to eat barbecue
and spin jagged circles
on the big black octopus
until the county boy
high on homegrown
pulled back the handle
at the top of the arc
and let the thing
slowly bump
and hiss
to a stop.

looking down,
spinning backwards in the sky,
i watched a clown
behind a tent
slap a ticket lady
to her knees.
then jerk her from the straw,
press his face to hers,
and kiss her hard
on the mouth.

then the stoned county boy
squeezed the broomstick
forward
until the octopus howled
and raised its jointed legs.
and the big metal chairs,
heavy with children,
began to turn
against the southern sky.

falling asleep at the drive-in on route 11

somewhere late in the second feature
i nodded off in the four-door ford,
and that sixteen-year-old i used to be
just up
and opened the driver's side door,
to hop out for popcorn and soda.

then weren't you suddenly the cat's meow,
sitting there in our car with
those wide dark eyes,
all curled in the corner in pink angora
purring "hurry back, or baby'll get cold."

and didn't i skedaddle
through an ocean of cars,
plying tailfin and bumper across the lot,
right into the concession's boast and shove
and all those saturday night boys
whirling in fluorescent light.

some smoky farmboys packing homebrew and guns,
a couple of jocks from the football squad,
the makeout king in a borrowed cadillac
grinning big over a handful of crackerjacks, saying,
"i better get back to audrey now boys,
you know they put a prize
in every box."

and headed back with my cardboard holder
beneath the night and all of those stars,
weaving through rows of daddies' cars, all
shining and steaming and aimed at the screen,
tethered like boats to their speaker posts,
rolling in that deep blue light.

back to you
waiting there in your fresh lipstick,
with your sister's perfume
still damp behind your ear,
the moonlight losing its way in your hair
and my heart so loud
i couldn't hear a thing.

then the metal door speaker
began to crackle and buzz,
and that boy that i was
began to melt away.
and you—
no longer anchored in the past—
i sat watching your skin
growing thin and blue.

i watched your hair
turning white in my hand,
and i brushed the wisps away from your face.
and in those last few seconds
of angel-blue light,
i licked my lips
and stole first base.

cakewalk

in brownsburg, va
a mockingbird cocks and tilts
on a tricky black wire,
hoping for borrowed voice
in the sticky balance
of light before evening star—
the only streetlight
flickers to life above the firehouse.

the pickups come circling in,
gathering like moths
in the skunk-ripe curl of dusk,
releasing their charges
plump and scrubbed—
two hundred years of farmwife
bearing the day's work
in saran wrap and foil.

it is a passing craft
we do so well—
to spiral around these tables,
marking our numbered course
to the lazy fiddle and mandolin plink
of three-quarter time.
ten tries for a dollar
to sink our teeth into angelfood
at the wheel's last click.

in the dirt lot
the men are spitting and shuffling,
chugging the last few sips
before they head inside.

we too would love to tilt our heads
to the darkened paths and hollows
filling with dead-man's-breath,
to coo the dovenotes
of passing time,
to whistle back the night
rolling fiercely in
from the fields.

gator night in south carolina

before it filled with fifteen years of rain
this quarry mothered all the county's men,
birthed slabs of stone,
pushed out great chunks of earth
until the day
there was no more to give—
then the tin shacks and trucks just disappeared
and the sassafras and saplings dug in.

water will search out the greater vessel
and nothing stays empty for long—
in a lean and dusty county
a girl of twelve learns it well.
from the creeks that crossed our family farms
we gave back all we could
to the deep, healing fill.

sometimes we'd gather
beneath the full swell of the moon
in a game we played so many summer nights.
the wagon roads filled with pickups,
winding and bumping to the quarry's edge.
the bonfires splashed the firs with light.
i'd follow the boys to the water
and toe the safety of the greenstone ledge—

then plunge with a squeal
into the darkened mouth of the quarry pool.
our inner tubes and water wings
would hold us high in the warmer layers—
those things of air that kept us safe,
that suspended us,

drifting and splashing,
above the black and soundless bottom.

until the gators came with their callused paws—
our fathers and brothers and uncles,
farmers and handymen all—
who slipped from the banks to the steaming shallows
and stroked their way to our sides.
who rose up from the blackness
and set upon us
with an unshaven and whiskied howl.

to feel the animal rush of being tipped
and eaten alive in the churn!
the strange desire for the heavy hand
that closes around your ankle,
that pulls you under,
that lets you bob free—
shrieking for more and more
again and again.

and all around
the delicate ghosts of the day
were steaming up from the water,
lifting into the thick summer air
in an arabesque
that always spidered off
to blackness.
just beyond the treeline
the double-e's rumbled and wailed,
burning south to savannah in the night.

francis the diving mule

things never looked so tiny up here—
as though all that carnival spinning
could shape the world,
and sugar was the only savior.

a mule will do that
at the end of a plank.
a mule like me and a two-by-four.

sometimes all the music in the world
can't make a monkey dance.
and in these days, stubborn as buttons,
wisdom can come in a flash.

an elephant on a peg.
a pig on a bike.
jesus—lemurs!

off in the east, what trees were fading.
oh, we could have climbed down then,
could've had a fat sandwich
and gotten sticky blue all night.

farmers, step right up.
and whistle in
them dogs...

but the horizon kept shifting
from minute to minute.
there was barley to be winnowed,
there were books to be read.

the holy
just need
a good splashing!

the gold changes hands at the hurdy-gurdy,
the music tickles your ears.
you just pray that the parson brought enough water.
you snort, and step off the edge.

the mouse game

don't worry about the mouse.
the mouse will be fine.
everybody lines up quarters
and i put mine on blue.
you put yours on red.

he's a spunky little fellow
in a wooden rainbow pie,
and i should have known
that you'd choose red— mainly
because you said you'd choose yellow.

the mouse will pick a hole
to duck into at the end.
only one of us can win, but
we're both still gonna play—
either way, the mouse gets fed.

the barker rings the bell
and he gives the pie a spin.
the mouse starts skipping and
i grin across the wheel—
when i win you're gonna feel like hell.

it's a kangaroo rat really.
real mice don't dance.
your glance across the table tells me
all i need to know—
you're leaving. it's just a matter of when.

but the mouse smells the chow
and now he's starting to twitch.
when we get back to the car
you'll be bitching and moaning
about every little thing, like you do

but look— his toes are tickling blue,
i've got you whipped by a mile.
come to papa, little mouse,
we've been waiting all night—
you and me are going out in style.

giant gorilla

on the last night in town
the carnival's open till midnight—
way past bedtime
for the hardwood loggers,
long-distance truckers, and
the men who plow earth into rows.
they've long since gone,
the parking lot is empty,
the fairhands are
starting to pack things away—
time to close up the show for the fall.
your husband
left three hours ago.

but we still haven't won
anything all night.
we've been wandering the fairgrounds
from stand to stand,
trying hard to win just one prize—
playing cigarette ring-toss, the skee-ball game,
even those floating, numbered ducks.
we're walking hand-in-hand now
since it's safe again,
but it's clear we're having
no luck at all.

there's a skinny, young guy
with a wallet chain
working the dart-throwing booth.
he's sipping a dr. pepper
and checking you out
so i decide… what the heck.
you're bound to win something
if you try long enough—
even you and i know that's true.
three darts for a dollar, to
hit balloons on a wall,
and prizes everywhere.

big green alligators,
purple bulls,
monkeys with long white fur.
boa constrictors wound around the rafters,
blue turtles all over the floor.
and then there's this giant gorilla,
all black and shaggy,
sitting in the middle of it all.
he's surrounded by
bears and stuffed pink panthers,
smiling, like he's the king
of the whole crazy show.

but just like everything else in life
the prize that you win
is actually hidden under the table.
it's a smurf doll keychain
or a white plastic puppy
wrapped up in cellophane.
"how many for the gorilla?"
i say to the guy,
who's still giving you that look.
i figure i know
what he's going through right now,
since i'm there, every day, myself.

maybe it's because
the carnival is closing
and he doesn't want to pack the gorilla away.
or maybe it's the way you take the darts
from his hand,
in the end, i'm not really sure.
but he leans back and grins,
says, "ten pops and he's yours, brother,"
his white teeth flashing in the light.
so i start tossing the darts,
you keep doing what you do,
and just like that
the gorilla is mine.

it's time to go.
we leave the carnival.
the gorilla rides in the back.
and we sit, mostly silent, in front
threading into the darkest mountains.
passing all those unlit farms
i keep thinking
about my wife, and you.
every time i look up
there are big white eyes
staring back
in the rear-view mirror.

i let you out
a half-mile from your place.
a quick kiss
and you disappear into the night.
for a second i think about going back,
then realize it's too late.
the road is deserted.
not a star or headlight.
it feels like I'm the last man alive.
the gorilla sits humped and black
in the back seat,
and seems to get larger
and larger as i drive.

smashing pennies

fish out your best one, put it on the tracks.
sacrifice something but make it small.
inhale diesel or creosote while you can.
if the lineman comes, hit the dust.

remember what you can of ryegrass, rust,
slag heaps. think of grease and smokestacks.
the changes are small, but criminal.
hoppercar skeletons, tankers, piggybacks.

an ear and steel are a tender match—
listen and you'll hear the wheels.
things like this you won't spend later,
and that thrumming is the coming of autumn.

if you think of value, spit it out.
consider ozone or the compression of air.
don't worry— you've got plenty of dimes,
and rainbows in the oil by your boots.

just kneel down here, at the edge of the tracks.
is this what you had in mind?
it's ok now, we're a good ways back.
relax. she's right on time.

dirt for sale

there was something about the hand-scrawled sign
that pulled us over to the side of the road

that caused us to pause in our country drive
and consider the earth in our idling.

the way we find ourselves outside.
the way we worm our way back in.

"stump grinder", "kittens", "honey", "live bait"—
opportunity waits around every bend,

but in the trailing light of a summer day
those things just curl out of sight.

here was a way to stake out a plot,
retake some ground we thought we'd lost.

a few bucks for the cost of burlap bags
five more for the guy with the shovel—

we attacked the pile at the back of the barn
heaping rich, black earth into the trunk of the car.

then when the trunk got full we started inside
and filled the backseat up to the roof.

we shoveled until the sun went down,
packed it in with our hands and knees,

then we pointed the heavy subaru home,
and headed back to the city.

it wrapped around us, like a sweater of earth,
pungent in the cool night air.

a mossy mound in the rear view mirror.
a dark presence, heaped just out of sight.

and craning around to check out the back
there was dirt sifting out of the half-open trunk,

dirt spilling out every window crack,
dirt spilling out around the doors.

there were clods exploding on the asphalt road
as the earth returned to itself—

our loamy trail on the road to home
and a chance to find our way back.

night driving

it takes an overnight trip on route 29
and a child with a head full of sleep

to scale the backseat of a white chevrolet
and climb way back into the stars.

stretched out long beneath the safety glass
the northbound lights melt around your head,

the trees skim past your toes in the dark
and all six cylinders are drumming through the night.

if you're lucky the radio brings in philadelphia
or chicago if the atmosphere's right—

murmuring voices from a faraway place,
your father's face in the instrument lights.

but that's impossible now. i've seen too many stars,
run too fast, down too many roads.

the things that you pass seem to pass you by later.
it gets harder to find your way home.

the pine trees still flash by in the headlights.
i roll down the window a crack—

but it's a different road when the wheel's in your hand.
and i'm too big to wedge myself back.

three

crossing the river in winter

february,
and any river
that would go hammering
down the gorge in spring
was widened and wedged
into either bank,
walk-on frozen, like never before—
the stillness and silence
always cruel
to those deceived
by the purity of white.

darkness
was just daring the west as well,
when we too emerged
through the murmur of cedar,
humped and arched with snow.
shouldering the silence
one flake at a time,
making our way
back to camp—
across the ice
to woodstove and stew,
as though heat
might somehow
become warmth again.

so,
near the middle—
when you stopped and turned,
as thin as winter.
when your voice was steaming
fur and ice—
were the sunfish circling
just below?
were the owls
lifting from the limbs?
was it
the center's thinness
favors neither shore,
or simply
i can't take this
anymore.

balance and the nitro house

whoever it was
that broke these mountains
like bread
and wound these emerald streams
around our smoking towns—
whoever it was that first dug deep
into the coal-black heart
of this land—
was pink-slipped and
packed off
long ago.

now,
it's the blood-red edge
of the mining ledger
that tugs at the sleeves
of our blackened men,
shouldering the weight
of the company store—
their seams and pockets
filled with dust,
and hope
burnt down to coke.

men who stand
before row after row
of horehound sticks
and peppermint
changing company scrip,

again and again,
into shotgun shells and wine
—then walk out, wondering
where it's all been spent,
while inside
the debt heaps higher.

men who in the end,
when they can't cough it up,
must send their daughters down here
to the nitro house.
where we will fill the vials
and hoist the pack
until their father's debt
is finally paid back,
in one or another way,
on the barefoot climb
back up to the maw
of the shaft.

the same dusty men
who are still surprised
at the first flat crack,
the shuddering sky,
and the thunderous roll that follows.
who rush headlong
into the storm outside
meeting their fears halfway—
and find only their sons,
streaked with rain,
bounding back
to the hearth
like echoes.

laid off

the last paycheck
bought a new tin stove.
it's good for cooking and heat.
i'll use it until the metal goes thin,
then sell it off while i can.
rust disappears under stoveblack,
then it's someone else's turn.
now i greet the day with an axe.

behind the trailer
in a stack of pine
i've learned to swing from the waist.
learned to splinter and split
until the axe head shrieks,
and my shoulders steam
in the cold.
i no longer have an old man's back.

lightwood goes fast
but heats like the devil.
the air hangs hot beneath the bulb.
all day i tease the kindling in, slow,
till it cracks into flame.
i stoke the stove
until the sky is smoke.
i try, but can't burn it all.

by nightfall
the stove is a bright red beast
that growls and sputters on the floor.
i spit— it dances on the stove like a dying man.
it dances long after my back has turned.
i pick up the axe
and slip outside.
i am hungry for something to burn.

breakfast at the pancake house on 29

it's one of those games
that looks real simple:
fifteen holes in a triangle board
and fourteen pegs,
the color of milk,
each one with its own little hole.

"i told you to quit smoking those things"

but there's the one hole extra,
and that's the trick.
that's what makes it a game.
you can set up the pegs
any way that you want,
but that hole's gotta be in the right place.

then you make your first move,
and start jumping the pegs,
tossing your jumps in the cup.
the object here
is to jump every little peg,
and end up right where you started.

"ok, smoke it dammit, or put it away"

memorize your moves,
anticipate the space.
you do what you have to do—
but you gotta be sitting
in the exact same place
when you finally get to the end.

if you end up with three pegs,
then you're "just so-so."
two, then you're "really smart."
but if you end up with one,
in the hole where you started,
you're a "genius."
and you play again.

cats

the cats were milkhouse-sleeping all day—
curled in the hay and out of the heat,
while the big silver separator
sweated and purred
and the concrete cracked outside.

down by the lake the fishing was slow,
but the drinking was good as it got.
the boys sipped and whittled away
while the afternoon stretched out hot and long
and the cane tips never once stirred.

night came creeping from the corner of the loft
as the sun lapped the last of the light from the sky.
downstairs, the hired man coughed and spat,
set down the pail to scratch his neck,
watched the cats as they slipped outside.

at eight, the bulb in the barn went black.
the hired man slid the barn door back
and, late for supper and sleep again,
set off down the lane beneath the wide, dark sky
and a sharp little claw of moon.

the empty bottle slid across the pickup truck floor.
the four boys on the seat just rolled with the curves
in a single-headlight swerve for home,
and they didn't even hear the hired man's yowl
when the bumper kissed him goodnight.

but the taillight caught the flicking tails,
the ears on-the-prick, and the eyes like glass.
the hired man stared up at the moon on its back.
he heard something glide from the grass by the road.
padding over to his side, it began to purr, then lap.

halloween

treat
the ghosts
of the almost-past
with a little more respect—
those vaporous trails that
drift from the parks
to reclaim the streets
in whispers.
the shiver
just
at the cusp
of darkness
when the red has
drained from the sky.
the shadow that flicks
at the corner of your eye
before the night
wolfs down
the moon.

check
the light
on the back
of your hands—
change is fast when it comes.
something's already clawing
at the dirt in the park.
the next howl
might be
your
own.
there's a
skeleton crew
out on the streets tonight,
a shadow across the bricks.
better stay away from
the eye of the moon—
get home before
you get
tricked.

waking in a basement on the first day of spring

winter coughed up spring
on its way to the shelter
but never quite made it
past the package store—

now there're four baggy kids
with a black baseball bat
just looking for
something to hit.

and mac's on the corner
selling roses for a fix,
scratching and rocking
and scratching his arms.

and kiki charms the silver
from some safeway change,
swinging slow down the street
in the heat.

the haitians are smoking
by their purple voodoo cabs
checking the exhausted street
for fares.

and no one cares that there're roses
for a dollar a bunch,
or that a big boombox
is pumping a hip-hop beat,

or that i've punched my way out
of this hibernation,
and up to the street
once again.

it's a day you can dance to—
everyone's thirsty,
and the liquor store
opens at ten.

monkeymind

it was quite a time to be under the trees—
meditating in a businesstown park
just bees and bark and some guardian angels
marking turf in their red berets.

heartworks— an occasional hazy fallump
tethered inside a spring machine.
i was barefoot and all, with no picnic chips,
when her photo popped from a honeydew magazine.

if a monkey drops from a tree in the city,
generally no one expects its arrival.

survival instinct slapdashes plans
and the time for hiving's later.
better tend to the tangerines,
leave protection to the pros.

the shouting's out loud and
damn the clothing. who even
knows the monkey calculus?

he was all messy and hopped-up,
getting furious and funky.
then furry screeches, more
furry screeches!

i'm curious as all getout
but a monkey just does
what a monkey sees.

big simian stacks
of sugar packs.
cherubim
and paraffin.

hairy leprechaun!
ketchup!
beeswax!

a man, his wife, and the television

a man loved his wife
and one day she died.
no, wait.
a man almost never watched television.
but sometimes
the man and his wife
watched television in bed.
she was beautiful and blue.
the light zipped across her face
and her hair was staticky red.
all night the television watched
them sleeping.
a man almost never watched his wife.
no, wait.
a man loved his television
and one day it died.
all night his wife watched
him sleeping.
it turned her on
the way the light from the screen
spilled across his face
like an underwater carnival in blue.
one night she turned off the set
and she died.
no wait.

a man almost never loved his wife.
one day she turned off the television,
walked into the hall,
the light pinpointed,
and he died.
no, wait.
once a man loved his television
that's all.

mrs. thurston

buildings grow taller
when it starts to rain.
i've felt it.
i know it's true.
it's dark here now
but down there in the park
the lights will shudder on
like they always do—
sparking out into the night
across all those cars
on their slowcrawl home
to their beds.

i know this
without opening my eyes.

and of course he's dead.
i know that too.
though you tried to replace him
with cheap glass and frame
i saw through it
right away.
i saw him reared back and fanning
his wings like a swan
in the air above my head—
felt the wind
crackle blue
through my hair.

you think i'm mad,
i know that you do.
the way i sit here
and knit
all night.
but purling the world
from my cats-hair skein
lets you stretch and snore
until dawn.

and when you burst back in
with your bright red smiles
i won't
be gone like before.
i've unplugged the lamps
and unscrewed
all the bulbs.
there's electricity
all over the floor.

the devil beating his wife

— old folk saying

the storm came down the river
like a bad husband,
banging from mountain to mountain,
bloated and mumbling something black.
low-slung clouds
hanging like fists in the heat.

and summer, on her back
on a red plastic raft,
floats with her toes in the drink.
the sun beating down.
a green dragonfly.
and pretty much nowhere to hide.

god i hate it
when he's like this, she thinks.
her arm glistens in the light.
she wonders about closing her eyes
and slipping under.
ponders leaving for good
in the fall.

thunder. lightning.
he's squalling in the treetops,
cracking the air like a whip.
heat and darkness mixing to silver.
and summer
toweling off on the bank

remembers the bedroom windows—
all wide open.
now there'll be hell to pay.
she's hoping
it won't take too long this time.
the first droplets hitting
her face.

new silk dress

you escaped
for the day, and now
you're standing here,
on a wobbly wooden box
in the rose's store,
down at the end of main street.
there's a three-way mirror,
some country muzak,
and a fluorescent buzz all around.
it's good to be out of the heat.

over on aisle four,
your two youngest ones
are playing with the plastic toys.
one boy's got a blue army-man
that looks just like his daddy.
the other's got a big, red,
water–powered rocket.
if you fill it up
and pump it hard enough,
it takes off into the sky.

but here's a spring-green dress,
green as a lawn,
clinging to your waist
like a brand new day.
and you standing in the spotlight—
palm-smoothing
slow.

corner of the eye,
breasts to bruised thigh—
imagining it all
a different way.

you begin to turn
in front of the mirrors,
and the dress
swings out all around.
it makes a rustling sound
like wind through the trees
when a rocket's
getting set
to launch.

you turn even faster
looking in the mirror,
to find something
you've never seen before—
an army of you
all stretched out behind,
standing tall and green,
spinning
like you went on forever.

and now you imagine
holding tight
to that water-rocket
as it whooshes up and
out of the back yard.
it climbs higher and higher,
way up above the house,
spewing water
all over the lawn.

and it seems like a hundred,
no, a thousand of you
spinning around
and cheering you on.
they're all lined up in mirrors,
trailing out for miles,
as you rocket upwards, leaving
the whole town behind.

and then you look back down
from your twirling in the sky,
to see the girl
turning on the box
at rose's.

you see the green silk dress,
the kids in the yard,
and all the things that
the girl thought she'd hidden.
and her husband standing small
at the edge of the patio,
staring up into the sun.
wondering how
he could have possibly done
all the things
that he did.

a morning like this

requires special care.
one where
what you know,
or barely,
is covered in mist.

where to begin
when there is no
horizon.
how far to go
when you know
you'll be lost.

this room
seems small.
the air
tastes like ginger
and the birds
in the trees
are silent.

yesterday
in the garden
four yellow crocuses,
a small snake trapped
in an empty
fountain.
i fell in love
with my mother.

four

eight pale women

for twenty years
i entered the ancient portals
of someone's *notre dame*
and tried to suspend,
to cross over,
to bathe in that warm
and beckoning current.

for twenty more
i watched from my red cushion.
watched the lotus petals fall
and drift downstream,
past a hundred water-filled bowls
where a silver moon reflected all
save mine.

for three days
i stood naked in the desert,
howled and danced
and rattled at the sky
while a vulture sun
circled overhead,
baking and cooling
my heart to terra-cotta.

in the yucatan
the feathered *musicas*
work their gold
into jaguars and bats

and scatter them across the andes.
the *trainos* tickle their throats
with ivory spatulas
to purge themselves pure for their gods.
while i rock and totter
behind the glass,
and look out across
this garden of shadows.

yesterday
at the edge of the woods
eight women,
pale and uninvited,
appeared and whispered,
"come with me" —
eight pale women
gauzed,
and carved
like ivory.

thin, thin life
i have dreamed you so.

tonight

we sleep.
in dryness, the knowledge of rain
    the moisture of lips?

a tumbling sky and a flash
    the rush
        and swerve
of sparrows

    one mississippi
    two mississippi

and what seems to come on so swiftly
        simply one
of a hundredthousand beats
crossing over.

i close my eyes
i close your eyes
we awaken in rain.

        the rain the same
    your lips, the rain
the same.

beach glass

since you left
i have been combing the shallows
for sea-smoothed glass,
scuffing the shoreline
with an eye for sparkle
and a sky-blue mason jar,
hoping to capture
the fragments of color
before they return
to sand.

out past the breakers,
beneath the hiss and surge,
the last chunks of a bottle
hit bottom.
sharp and persistent
they are lifting and falling,
shattering and rolling
into jewel.

all afternoon
i find turquoise and jade
in the shallows
behind the house,
wading back and forth
and back again,
making sure
that nothing is missed.

and back on the sill
in our new sunroom
are three jars
i've already filled.

late in the day
if the sun is just right
the light spills across
the walls, like waves.
the water crests high
above my head.
the room
heaves,
and rights itself
again.

a darkening kitchen

what does it mean
to capture anything in a picture
when the spirit
will always escape?
will break from the border
of the polaroid print,
or seep through the cracks
of the frame.

picture this:
your hair
tousled
like the waves we're crashing
three gulls circling
and a flag snapping behind.

or this:
a pewter bowl
of green grapes and a pear
mottled apples
and a backyard fig
in a halo of gold leaf.

draw close the chairs
and we will talk all night
over bittersweet cider.
of the way the waves recede.
of the orbits of grapes and lovers.
of the gulls
spiraling off
to the west.

a cowskull and georgia o'keeffe

i have seen your kind before,
standing tall
and draped in black,
flashing back
at a world
that won't stay still.

even as
you cradle my skull
like a loaf of bread
or the child
you never had,
my broad back rises,
still shouldering the sky
against your turquoise hills.

these sockets you finger
hold globes
that you can never know.
these nostrils
cracked and chipped
still bellow and snort
in the furnace air.
still echo along the ridges.

the coyote shadow
still paws my bones,

picked and sucked
and dragged off long ago,
and the scorpion
kicks and claws
in my dust.

but i was the stroke
long before
you ever raised the brush.
and in the end,
i am the poem
before
you lift the pen.

the walnut tree waits for its bees

before the day's first return
lies a long, hot stretch
of something like fear.
fear that says
maybe this is the time
that they finally move on.
maybe this time they've gone for good
— swarming off through the woods
and past the hilltop,
disappearing in specks.

it is hard to wait all day.
harder still to stay rooted,
with fields of cloverbud
away and just out of sight.
thinking one might, with the wind *just so*
and a loamy groan,
move from the pines
through these slats of light
and into a brilliant plain.

you should know
that those scouts are mine.
earned through ring after ring of rain,
earned in slow and spreading loss
from the inside out.
and so too i have earned
their gifted returns.
and how drop by droplet
the hollows are filling
with a cool and sticky balm.

pomegranate

autumn slipped in
through the wither and crackle
bearing fruit
of a sweeter season—
a swollen pod
of deep red pearls
each glistening
with the promise
of change.

tonight
i will lick my bare shoulder
and rock myself
to sleep.
lips parted like petals,
tongue slick
with the taste
of the season to come.

oyster

I.
the crunch of sand
under black rubber boots
and the flash of steel
in light unfamiliar.
the flip and glide of mullet
and the slow fanning of the shark
with its hangman's eye—
things sensed, not seen.
drawn in
let out
and drawn back again.
the world is filtered
through flesh.

II.
open wide
on a broken hinge.
exposed and spread out
on a swirling bed of
silver, blue and green.
a fleshy pink, tinged in black,
that stirred desire
in the bellies of kings.
i slip two fingers
beneath the still warm folds
and lift the oyster to my mouth—
surprised by the sea
returning.

III.
bulbs and pods
risen from the kelp,
razor clam and tiger's eye,
shark's tooth and sun-bleached claw—
some things the sea gives freely,
some must be taken.
knee-deep in the dark blue swirl
the oystermen are prowling
in hip boots and mitts.
patient as angels,
tracing mercury wakes.
steel for prying and
steel for crushing.
oak, the judgment staff.
green wicker, the grave.

IV.
last night
i turned sailor
on a rolling deck,
was lifted and tossed
to the waiting sea.
i struck the surface
with a crack and shattered,
fragments scattered
across the waves
to fall dusting, drifting
through a cobalt eye.
phosphorous ghosts

in silent descent,
settled across
a lightless floor—
where you waited then
on an alabaster bed,
to suck me into
a slippery mantle,
and roll me
slowly
to pearl.

sky-clad

the night of your hands
requires wall-to-wall sky—
something more than desert
spread out beneath the heat.

here, the distance
between stellar blue dahlia
and the tip of my tongue
isn't simply a subtraction
of black silk.

and the tracery of perseid,
and the so-soft moon,
is nothing to the slide
of your lips

down here,
the santa anas pick up,
moaning something like morning.
and we awaken, stars
in each other's mouth.

my muse

wouldn't give you
the time of day.
and anyway
she doesn't live around here.
she calls up
says, "hey bug" or, "hey turnip"
or, "hello little dear."
"i'm here at the hilton.
be down by eight,
and don't be late."
and before i can answer,
click, she's off,
and i'm sitting
with the cordless
in my hand.

my muse
she stands about five foot six.
combat boots
and thick black shades,
with that sexy-anorexic
just-off-the-jet tilt
that's deadly at any speed.
that one call
is all i need, and
i'm off downtown
dropping valet dollars and
punching buttons—
till she opens the door,

sighs, "you obviously missed me.
l.a. was dreadful.
shut up and kiss me."

my muse
she never
takes no for an answer.
the "do not disturb" sign
is swinging from the door,
before i know it
i'm dancing backwards to bed,
the bath is steaming and
the loofah's waiting,
she's got caviar heading
to the twentieth floor.

tomorrow i know
i'll wake up alone—
she'll have flown off
to greece or somewhere.
but tonight it's alright
because whenever she comes,
my muse
always leaves me
speaking in tongues.

le cadavre exquis at the villa la rocca

guard dogs snarl and bark at the sky
and the vineyards darken in the east.
thunder approaching.
and a quickening in the air.
the leaves bare their throats to the wind.

in this blue hour
we light thick candles
and push our chairs together.
there is red wine, bread
and a heavy table
to keep the darkness at bay.

we've felt you watching,
exquisite corpse,
from where you wait
at the top of the stairs.
we uncork the bottles
and raise the glasses,
our eyes reflecting the light.

surely this place is haunted
by the living,
and our thoughts of what might be:
the pen and paper,
the angle of light,
how a form will curve
through the eye of a lens,
endless with possibility.

more thunder,
then rain begins to fall
down through the *eye of god.*
the marble is slick and cool in the hall,
candles illumine those who came before,
and the pedestal waits for us all.

in the stone hallways
darkness is gathering.
it spirals with you down the stairs.
exquisite corpse,
with your fingers like moths
and hair like water,
your wrists
translucent to the bone.

then lightning
rising up from the village below
and cracking the clouds into red.
this is ancient language
between earth and god—
no one here has anything to add.

out back
the dogs glide by on wires
and claw their own paths in the dirt.
the things that protect us
and keep us alive
can also rip us to pieces.

but, now you are with us,
behind the chairs,
your skin as pale as the moon.
the back of your hands
glowing
like embers at the edge of the room.

each of these stories begins anew,
as we pass from hand to hand—
but always
it ends up the same.
if you look at me,
i unfold like paper.
you touch me,
i envelop in flame.

night writing

nodding to the a.m. scrabble of airwaves
in a month of pencil shavings and tax returns

the night dj vanishes uh-one more time
the needle lifts, the belt creaks, the arm returns

now at the dead-set middle of midnight
the yard tilts westward, begins its return

how is it these scratchings take the shape of a man
and the men line up, expecting all in return?

or say, the way that a hand falls open on the desk
when there's nothing left to return

something like diamond spiraling to spindle
tells you flatly: there can be no return

the pen finger taps. the disc spins again
the moment arcs to a point, and returns

creating trees

a sculptor stands beside a fallen tree,
hatchet and hammer in hand.
he hacks off the bark and begins to carve.
he chips and shaves all day.
the sun arcs over and the night comes on.
he stands back and sees a woman made of wood.

at that moment, a poet finishes her poem
in a room overlooking the woods.
it's not bad, she thinks,
as she closes her notebook.
the paper is rough
like the bark of a tree.
it is a poem about a sculptor's hands.

at night the trees begin to sway and creak.
the sculptor dreams of a tall white oak.
the poet is talking softly in her sleep—
her words rustle in the dark
like leaves.

morning,
and the poet opens the shutters
as the sculptor walks by with his axe.
he smiles
and she slowly backs away from the sill.
today she will write on the back of a leaf.
she will write in a pen with green ink.
whatever she thinks, she will write it down
until the last of the leaves has been filled.

today the sculptor does not fell a tree,
but climbs up into the low-hanging limbs.
he trims back the bark
and with delicate hands
begins scraping back cool, white wood.
he shapes and carves the curves of the branch
until he reaches the tips of the twigs.
he carves until the sky is dark.

the sculptor is sleeping
in a cradle of leaves
when the poet arrives at the base of the tree.
he opens his eyes, the tree has grown higher.
her face is as pale as the moon.

as soon as he wakes
the sculptor takes up his knife.
the poet lifts her pen to the tree.
already they see that the branches are changing,
there is life in the hollows and crooks of the limbs.
the trunk looks immense and
the leaves have turned silver.
they are shivering, falling and
swirling about.

the sculptor no longer
feels the work of the blade,
feels only the give and glide of change.
he finds that what he made was already there,

and that the tree has grown smooth and white.
in the light of the tree
his hair becomes vine,
trailing down to the earth.

and the pen of the poet
becomes a bouquet of blossoms.
she drops it, and it roots in the ground—
her words feather, and take flight.
the poet and the sculptor
stand back and watch them,
soaring up through the branches
like doves into the night.

the calligraphy of fireflies

summer had slumped off
over the lazy hill
like a struckout kid
and we were packing it up as well,
getting ready to make that graceless run
from home to our various colleges—
the first of many
leavings and returnings
that mask the breaks
made long before.

the wind we felt
at the edge of the woods
was more than a signal
of the season's end,
did more than send the cicada home
and set the duck wings spinning
in the yard.
it raised the flesh
along our arms, and
in the final innings
of backlot ball
brought the fireflies in swarms.

green and tenuous handfuls
scattered across
the uncertain outfields.
a staccato rhythm
of position and coaxing

blown like sparks
from some far-off blaze—
marking and re-marking
to disappear again
drifting
on their own dark currents.

so tonight,
while we shift and toss
in a punctured sleep,
calculating loss and gain,
we dream that
all we have gathered and scattered wild
will define itself
again and again—
a changing constellation
that roars and mutates
in the sky above our heads.
and deep into night
our rooms will glow
with a frenzied green
from the jars
beside our beds.

one meeting

a woman
slips
in and out
of her dreams
at will.

the cloud
is in
the paper,
so the tiger
is still
in the tea leaves.

from
dark eggs,
snow-
white birds.

About the Capital Collection

The Caoital Collection is a signature by The Word Works that features excellence in poetry from authors usually in the Greater Washington, DC area. The hallmark of this collection is that each book selected is financially supported by community contributions and advance book sales. The following individuals have contributed to the Capital Collection to make this book possible:

PATRONS:

Robert E. Brailsford
Walt Clocker
Gene Colombini
Wendell Hawken
Rick & Becky Klein
Miles David Moore
Virginia Pauker
Ray Regan
Kenneth Schiciano
Hilary Tham
Larisa & Carl Wells

DONORS:

Karren L. Alenier
Nancy & Dan Allen
Scott & Sonja Beebe
Mel Belin
Ron Blasing
Ann Brewer Knox
Doris Brody
Jennifer Daniels
Pat Davis
John & Virginia Eaddy
Jeff & Susan Ebeling
Nicholas D. Etcheverry
Clarinda Harriss
Beverly Hines
Ted & Lori Humphrey
Myong-Hee Kim
Joanna & Steve King
Tom Kirlin
Marilyn Kravitz

Scott Lindlaw
Annie & Paul Mahon
Judith McCombs
E. Ethelbert Miller
Melanie Moro & Sami Ramadan
Peggy Osner Heller
Harold V. Pini
Mary Procter
Leslie Remencus
Tim Rogers
Mary Rozell
Joshua Silver
Jill Tunick
Charlotte Warren
Barry Wepman
Marcella Wolfe

FRIENDS: *John Ackerly*
Nancy Allinson
Barri Armitage
Dean Blehert
Maggie Briand
Grace Cavalieri
Meredith Cole & Peter Krebs
Sally Cranston
Don Cunningham
Lillian Frankel
Paul Grayson
Steve Hester
Susan Lesser
Elaine Magarrell
John B. Michener
Faye Moskowitz
Jane O'Leary
Justine Roeden
Steve Schaible & Kevan Miller
Millie Shott
Lori Stahl & Matt Caduff
Robert Thomas & Samantha Estergood
Jonathan Vaile

Special thanks to the anonymous Patrons, Donors and Friends who also
supported this book.

About the Word Works

THE WORD WORKS, a nonprofit literary organization, publishes contemporary poetry in collectors' editions. Since 1981, the organization has sponsored the Washington Prize, a $1,500 award to an American poet. Monthly, Word Works presents free literary programs in the Chevy Chase Café Muse series, and each summer, free poetry programs are held at the historic Joaquin Miller Cabin in Washington, DC's Rock Creek Park. Annually, two high school students debut in the Miller Cabin Series as winners of the Young Poets Competition.

Since 1974, WORD WORKS programs have included: "In the Shadow of the Capitol," a symposium and archival project on the African-American intellectual community in segregated Washington, DC; the Gunston Arts Center Poetry Series (Ai, Carolyn Forché, Stanley Kunitz, among others); the Poet-Editor panel discussions at the Bethesda Writer's Center (John Hollander, Maurice English, Anthony Hecht, Josephine Jacobsen, and others); Poet's Jam, a multi-arts program series featuring poetry in performance; a poetry workshop at the Center for Creative Non-Violence (CCNV) shelter. Master Class workshops (Agha Shahid Ali, Thomas Lux, Marilyn Nelson) and the Arts Retreat in Tuscany are ongoing programs.

In 2003, WORD WORKS will have published 51 titles, including work from such authors as Deirdra Baldwin, J.H. Beall, Christopher Bursk, John Pauker, Edward Weismiller, and Mac Wellman. Currently, Word Works publishes occasional anthologies and books under three imprints: the Washington Prize, the Capital Collection and International Editions.

Past grants have been awarded by the National Endowment for the Arts, National Endowment for the Humanities, DC Commission on the Arts & Humanities, Witter Bynner Foundation, Writer's Center, Bell Atlantic, Batir Foundation, and others, including many generous private patrons.

THE WORD WORKS has established an archive of artistic and administrative materials in the Washington Writing Archive housed in the George Washington University Gelman Library.

Please enclose a self-addressed, stamped envelope with all inquiries.

The son of an English teacher and a dairy farmer's daughter, James C. Hopkins grew up as a "faculty child" on the campus of an all-male boarding school in Lynchburg, Virginia. He received a B.A. in French Language and Literature from Duke University and began working as an investment broker in New York City. He has worked in that profession for the past 19 years.

In 1992, he received a Jenny McKeane Moore scholarship for poetry at George Washington University, to study with poet John Haines, and has been writing and performing his poetry since. His work has appeared in many literary journals and anthologies, including *Potomac Review, Minimus, Frantic Egg,* and *WordWrights!,* and his chapbook, *The Walnut Tree Waits for Its Bees,* was published by Mica Press in 1997. This is his first full-length book of poetry.

Photo by Marni P. Kravitz

With an interest in Eastern religions and cultures, James and his partner Marni spend much of their time traveling in Asia. For the past six years, they have lived on an old wooden boat in the Potomac River, and have just recently returned to land.